IF YOU HAVEN'T GOT THE **TIME** TO DO IT **RIGHT,** WHEN WILL YOU FIND THE **TIME** TO DO IT **OVER?**

Jeffrey J. Mayer

A Fireside Book
Published by Simon & Schuster

New York
London
Toronto Sydney
Tokyo Singapore

Fireside
Simon & Schuster Building
Rockefeller Center
1230 Avenue of the Americas
New York, New York 10020

First Fireside Edition 1991
FIRESIDE and colophon are registered trademarks
of Simon & Schuster

Designed by Barbara Marks Graphic Design
Manufactured in the United States of America

10 9 8 7 6 5 4 3
10 9 8 7 6   Pbk.

Library of Congress Cataloging in Publication Data
Mayer, Jeffrey J.
   If you haven't got the time to do it right, when will
you find the time to do it over? / Jeffrey J. Mayer.
      p. cm.
   1. Time management.   I. Title.
HD69.T54M39   1990
650.1—dc20   90-30065
                                            CIP

ISBN 0-671-69490-1
ISBN 0-671-73364-8 Pbk.

To my wife, Mitzi,
and my daughter, DeLaine;
both of whom I love very much.

CONTENTS

The 1990s—Living and Working in a Pressure Cooker

Improving productivity has become the rallying cry of the '90s. Fierce competition, both at home and from abroad, is forcing every company to streamline its operations and search for other ways to increase productivity. More work is being done by fewer people, and the burden has fallen on all of us. Management expects us to become more productive and complete more work in less time. Because we need to spend extra hours at the office to get the job done, we come in early, stay late, and work weekends. Nobody works a forty-hour week; fifty to sixty hours is the norm. But are we really increasing our productivity, or just the number of hours we work?

Adding to the burden, American business has spent billions of dollars on telecommunications systems so that information can be transmitted at faster and faster speeds. Information is sent and received instantly; a reply is expected immediately. There is electronic mail and voice mail, fax machines, beepers, and car phones. The computer at

work talks to the one at home. It's impossible to read, study, or even open all the letters, reports, magazines, books, newspapers, and computer printouts that cross our desks. There's no longer time enough to think, plan, or ponder a problem before being forced to make a decision. We're overloaded with information and are being over-whelmed with work.

With so much to do and so little time in which to do it, we try to stretch the length of our days, and hope that there will be just a little time left over for family and friends. But the hours at the office keep getting longer; the demands, pressures, strains, and tensions keep growing. Our goals and dreams are still unfulfilled. Clearly something is wrong.

A Typical Day

You get up early, hurry to the office, talk on the telephone, look at the mail, shuffle papers from one pile to another, and don't accomplish much. There are constant interruptions. The phone is always ringing, or someone is knocking on the door, asking, "Have you got a minute?" You attend unimportant meetings that take too long and leave issues unresolved. When you finally start to do some work, you are forced to drop everything in order to put out someone else's fire. *Important* things are constantly being pushed aside for whatever is most *urgent.* You go from one crisis to the next, and when it's finally time to go home—usually with a briefcase stuffed with papers you didn't have time to look at in the office—you're exhausted. There's just too much to do and never enough time. You're busy, but are you productive?

Life, and work, doesn't have to be this way. The key to solving all these problems is not simply to work longer and harder. We can't. There just aren't any more hours in the day, or days in the week. We're all facing the woodsman's dilemma:

> There was a woodsman who had a new ax. The first day he was able to chop down twenty trees. With each passing day, he worked longer and harder, while chopping down fewer trees. A friend wandered by and suggested, "Why don't you sharpen your ax?" The woodsman replied, "I'm too busy. I've got to chop down more trees!"

Let's stop for a moment, collect our thoughts, and sharpen our axes.

There Is a Solution—Get Organized!

How often have you said to yourself, "I just wish I had more time"—time to think about and analyze a problem, or even a few extra minutes to lean back in your chair and clear your head before you tackle your next project? Unfortunately, you can't stop the clock—it keeps ticking. But there's one thing you *can* do that will give you precious extra minutes: *Save time by wasting less of it!*

Hours of valuable time are wasted every business day. You're trained to save paper clips and reuse file folders (they cost the company money and are valuable). But time is even more valuable, so why waste it? Become better organized and you can convert the time that's now wasted during a normal business day into time that can be used more productively and effectively. Getting organized will also help you keep up with the overload of information, stay one step ahead of the competition—and go home a winner.

This book will show you how to save time and use it more effectively. The ideas, concepts, and techniques are simple and are mostly common sense. You've probably heard many of them before but were always too busy to implement them. We've all attended time-management seminars and walked away with great ideas, but when we returned to the office there would be a dozen telephone messages and another six inches of mail. Those ideas were never put to good use. The seminar was another waste of time and money.

I've spent much of my life searching for ways to get more work done in less time. I've worked with hundreds of businessmen and -women, and have developed techniques that have helped them save at least an hour of precious time each day—time they were able to use to make better business decisions worth thousands, even millions of dollars in profits for their companies. These same techniques will get you organized, help you save time, and make you more money. You'll be more productive at work and have extra time to enjoy your life away from the office.

You'll be amazed at how your productivity will increase

simply because you've made modifications in your work habits. Don't expect this to be easy. It'll take some effort on your part to get organized, but the rewards—in time and money—will be well worth it. And after you've put my timesaving techniques into practice, they'll be very easy to maintain.

Years ago, I was asked a simple question: "Jeff, which do you value more, pleasing habits or pleasing results?" I was trapped and began to squirm. Sheepishly I said, "Pleasing results."

From that point on I began to look at my work differently. Many of the things I did—as well as the things I observed—were just "pleasing habits." I began to question everything I did. In some cases I found I acted as I did simply because "That's the way we do it around here." In others I had gotten into a routine. It had never crossed my mind to do things differently. I wanted better results, though, so I changed my habits.

Change is never easy, and we resist it. But I've learned that we often make things harder for ourselves than we need to. Many of the daily obstacles that get in our way are put there by us. This book will show you how to overcome those obstacles, get everything done, and still have time left over for yourself.

You won't save time by looking for it in large blocks; look for it in small pieces instead. *Save thirty seconds every five minutes, and by the end of the day, you've saved an hour.* If you put the timesaving ideas, tips, and techniques in this book into practice, I guarantee that you'll save at least an hour of precious time a day.

The first part of the book shows you how to organize your *work space*—your desk, your files, and your office. The second part offers tips and techniques you can use to streamline the routines and responsibilities of your *business day*—all the way from meetings to mealtimes.

Getting organized is a step-by-step process. It may seem

awkward and uncomfortable at first, but with a little practice, you'll feel as if you've been doing it all your life. It's like learning how to ride a bicycle. At first you wobbled all over the sidewalk and fell down a few times. With practice you began to get the hang of it, and in no time you were riding full speed, with no hands.

My timesaving tips and techniques will help you get where you want to go in today's fast-paced and demanding business world. Why keep spinning your wheels and riding in circles, when you can achieve all your goals with time to spare?

PART I

MAKE YOUR DESK
WORK FOR YOU

The Perils of a "Pilamaniac"

You've probably seen offices that look as if they'd gone through the spin cycle of a washing machine, or as if a dump truck had backed up and dropped its load. There are piles of papers everywhere: on the desk, on the credenza, on the floor and couch. There are newspapers; magazines; books; pink phone slips; yellow, blue, and green Post-it notes; pads and pads of paper; new files; used files; colored files. Then there are papers—big pieces, little pieces, new pieces and old pieces.

How can a person get any work done with such clutter? Most of those papers probably aren't even needed. The person who sits behind that desk may *look* busy, but is the job really getting done? Think of the time wasted just trying to find something in all that mess.

There's a reason for cluttered desktops and piles of files: *Out of sight is out of mind*. We're afraid to put anything away, because we know we'll never find it again, or we'll forget about it. By leaving everything out, we can see all

our unfinished work. It's right there in front of us, spread out all over the desktop. Unfortunately, everybody else can see it, too.

There are lots of different ways to make a pile. Some of us like square piles, with all the corners nice and neat. Others prefer big mounds of papers. Sometimes there are numerous little piles that grow like anthills all over the desk. Or there is just *the pile*, an enormous growth of things coming out of the center of the desk.

One of my favorites is the pile that's laid out like a deck of cards in a game of solitaire. Obviously, making a pile like this takes a lot of practice and patience. The top of each piece of paper is exposed so the name or title can be seen.

When everything has all been laid out, the pile can grow to several feet in length and contain dozens of papers. It looks great on the desk—nice, neat, and efficient—but the work never gets done.

Many people like to pile their papers in stackable trays. That way they can use the air rights above their desks for storage. Sometimes these trays grow five, six, or seven tiers high, which creates considerable excitement. As the trays grow higher and the weight of the papers gets heavier, they start to bend in the middle and bulge at the sides. You begin to wonder if they will collapse and come crashing down when one more piece of paper is added, like the balsawood bridges you made in high-school science class, testing their strength by placing weights on them until they collapsed.

Are You a "Pilamaniac"?

Take a look at your desk. What do you see? Better yet, what *don't* you see? If only little patches of the top of your desk are visible, you are suffering from pilamania. You're not using your desk as it was meant to be used. You're not working as efficiently and productively as you could be. You're wasting valuable time. Eliminate that clutter and you'll save at least thirty minutes a day, simply because you'll be able to find all the unfinished work that has been lying around in piles, untouched, on your desk.

At least 60 percent of the papers piled on your desk no longer have any value or meaning. They've piled up because you were lazy. Instead of deciding what should be done with them, you've just put them in a pile. An example would be an invitation to attend a seminar or luncheon. Rather than make a decision right then and there, you put it aside—and it was quickly forgotten. The event will have probably taken place already by the time the invitation comes to the surface again.

When junk mail arrives, instead of tossing it immediately, you put it on the "I'll get to it later" pile, for when you have more time. Unfortunately, later never comes—and the pile gets bigger and bigger. You probably knew it was so unimportant that you didn't even bother opening it.

Many papers are sent for informational purposes. There are always people who feel that everyone in the office should read their memos and correspondence. They put everybody on the routing slip. Many of these things shouldn't even be sent to you, but you get them, and they end up on your desk—in a pile. Other papers have been on your desk for so long that the situation has taken care of itself or just gone away, but the papers still remain. All this clutter makes it more difficult for you to get your real work done and reduces your productivity.

You may *think* you know where everything is, but it takes a lot of time to find it—wasted time. The real danger comes when something of value or importance ends up buried in one of those piles. These unfinished projects, reports, and papers demand your immediate attention, and too often they are forgotten or lost. They'll remain undone until someone calls asking for the information, or you wake up in the middle of the night remembering some important project you never started. Now a crisis develops, and you have to drop everything and deal with it.

As the piles grow, it becomes more difficult to separate the important from the unimportant. It's almost impossible to decide what to do first.

> *Years ago I was standing in line waiting for an ice-cream cone. The man ahead of me asked for a bottle of apple juice. The salesgirl said, "Would you like strawberry-apple juice, banana-apple juice, or cranberry-apple juice?" The customer got confused, couldn't make a decision, and walked out.*

When you arrive at the office and have piles of papers all over your desk, you don't know where to begin.

There are so many choices, and all of them appear to be important. You become paralyzed. It becomes impossible to make a decision, and you start feeling guilty. You know what you should be doing but can't motivate yourself to get started.

You probably begin with the easy stuff, thinking you'll get in the mood, and after you get going you'll be ready for the important things. Unfortunately, it doesn't happen. You waste your valuable time and energy on trivia, and when you're finished, the meaningful and important work is still buried in a pile.

At some point you must do this work. You think you work better under pressure, so you start the project at the fifty-ninth minute of the eleventh hour, when your back is against the wall. You haven't left yourself any time to think. There's no longer a margin for error, a cushion, or room to maneuver. You're forced to shoot a bull's-eye when you're tired and your eyes are bloodshot. It takes a lot of hard work and effort even to see the target. You ultimately complete the project, but with a lot of effort, exertion, and overtime. The finished product isn't as good as it could have been, and the pressures of the deadline have taken their toll on you both physically and emotionally.

If you wait until the last minute to get your work done, you pay a price. Ultimately, you and your company will be faced with several expensive choices. Either you must work longer and harder, or the company will be forced to hire more people to take over some of this work—which increases overhead without increasing productivity. This costs everyone time and money.

There's a third choice (which most of us never pick): *Stop cold, drop everything, and get organized.* The issue isn't whether a desk is clean or messy. That's a smoke screen. The real issue is *time* and *money:* the quality of your work and the length of time needed to complete it.

With an organized, efficient desk, you can save both

time and money. Fewer things will slip through the cracks. You can stay on top of all your unfinished work, locate your papers and files within seconds, and become more productive. You'll look forward to coming to work in the morning, and you'll get home earlier at night. You'll feel better about your job—and you'll feel better about yourself.

The Moment of Truth: The Showdown Between You and Your Desk

You'll need about *two hours of uninterrupted time* to organize your desk, get rid of all those piles, and file the papers you want to keep. *Schedule an appointment with yourself.* There's no such thing as free time. *Write it on your calendar and keep the appointment. Close the door, turn off the telephone, and allow no interruptions. Bring a Dumpster.*

The whole process begins with the top of your desk. Take a look at every piece of paper in every pile. You may experience a mild shock in the process, coming across letters from people you haven't seen in years, memos and reports about projects that have long since been completed or abandoned. Your whole life may begin to flash before your eyes. Why are you keeping all this stuff? If you can't come up with a good answer, *get rid of it.*

Go through every paper in each pile and separate the papers you need to keep from the papers that can be thrown away. Pick up a piece of paper and look at it. If there's any work that needs to be done or action that needs to be taken, *keep it.* Start a pile of papers to keep. If you don't need it, *throw it away!*

In just a few minutes you've probably lightened your paper overload by more than half. Miraculously, you've transformed all those piles of files into just one stack of papers that you definitely need to keep. And you've thrown so much away that your wastebasket is overflowing and spilling onto the floor.

Creating and Using a Master List

Now the next step is to go through all the papers in the keeper pile and make a *Master List,* an inventory of all your unfinished work and ongoing projects. You'll be creating a new type of follow-up system—one based on a list instead of a pile.

Start with the paper on the top; pick it up, look at it, and ask yourself a simple question: *Is there any work that must be done?* Do I have to make a telephone call? Write a letter or a report? Give this to someone else? Am I awaiting a telephone call? A letter? Is there anything that remains undone? If so, *write it on your Master List.*

You now need to decide if it's necessary to keep this piece of paper. If the answer is no, throw it out. If the answer is yes, it should be put inside a properly labeled file. If a file doesn't already exist, make one up. But for the moment, just put it aside until we have discussed how to set up an efficient filing system.

Now that you have handled that first piece of paper, go

through all the papers one by one and repeat the process. If it's a piece of unfinished business, write it on your Master List. If you don't need to keep that piece of paper, toss it. If you do, put it aside to be filed.

The Master List you're creating is very similar to the index on your computer. You turn on the machine, push the proper button, and it displays a list of every file located within its memory. You select the file you want, push a button, and the machine displays the information on the screen. Imagine how much work it would be if you couldn't locate a specific file and were forced to search through every piece of information in the computer's memory. That's exactly what you are doing when you have to search through piles of papers on your desk. With your Master List, and your important papers properly filed, you will always know—in an instant—what has to be done and where to find the information necessary to do it.

How to Use Your Master List

There's nothing new about making lists. You've probably been doing it all your life—grocery lists, shopping lists, "things to do today" lists, New Year's resolutions. You may already have a *pile* of lists on your desk along with all the other piles.

Your Master List is different. Once you've made it, you're not going to tuck it away in your pocket or put it in a desk drawer and forget about it. You're going to refer to it and use it every minute of your workday. It will become your master plan for keeping track of your current tasks, as well as a reminder of what you have to do in the future. Never again will papers pile up on your desk. As soon as a memo, report, or letter arrives, you will look at it and make a decision.

■ If it concerns you, write it on your Master List
   and file it in the appropriate place.

- If it concerns someone else or someone else's job, send it on.
- If it's not important, get rid of it.

Your Master List will be the last thing you look at before you leave the office in the evening and the first thing you review when you arrive in the morning. You'll add new items as the day progresses, and cross off items when the jobs are done. Your Master List will become a measure of what you have accomplished today and a reminder of what you must do tomorrow and in the future.

Here are some tips on how to make and use your Master List:

- Your list should be written on a lined letter- or legal-size pad of paper. Never use small pieces of paper. You'll end up with piles of lists.
- Write on every line on the page, and do not number the items on the list. You're creating an inventory of all your unfinished work, not a numerical listing. These items are written at random, whenever you happen to pick up a piece of paper and make a note of it on the next empty line. When there aren't any more lines on the first page, start a second one. Priorities are not important at this moment. Just make sure that you get into the habit of writing everything down—then you won't need to remember it.
- You're not in the list business, so don't rewrite your list every day. You'll end up spending more time writing lists than doing work.
- When you finish a project, give yourself the pleasure of crossing that item off your list. Don't just put a check by it; draw a line through it. You'll derive a great deal of satisfaction from doing that.

- When you've completed about 50 percent of the items on the first page of your list, transfer the unfinished work to the next page. Cross off the items as they are being transferred. Take one last look at the old list to make sure everything was either done or transferred, so that nothing slips through the cracks. If you need to keep your old lists, make a file labeled ''Old Lists.''
- Date your lists. That way you can see how long some unfinished items of business have been there.
- Use a ballpoint pen. Pencils tend to smudge, and felt-tip pens with broad points are often illegible.
- Keep your Master List on top of your desk during the day, where you can see it. Don't put it inside a file folder.

While you're going through all your piles of files and making a list of all your unfinished work, don't be surprised to find that there are a lot of things you haven't done. Your Master List could easily be two or three pages long. Many people become terrified when they see all their unfinished work staring back at them on a seemingly endless list. They feel fear and guilt all at once—fear because there are important projects on the list that could lead to a crisis if they aren't completed immediately, and guilt because of all the things that were promised and never delivered.

The sad truth is that some people always feel very comfortable surrounded by their piles of files. All those papers give the illusion that work is being done, even if it isn't. They create a sense of security. However, it's false security! Take away the piles and these people feel naked and vulnerable.

You, too, may feel a little uncomfortable at first with a

desk that looks like the flight deck of an aircraft carrier
instead of a toxic-waste dump—especially since it took only
two hours to make the transition. Everyone in your office
will think you just quit, and you're going to be experiencing a bit of a culture shock. All those papers and files made
you feel important, and you could brag about how busy
you were. At least you *looked* busy. Now it looks as if you're
out of a job.

Let's consider the real purpose of your desk. It exists for
you to get your work done. You have two specific needs:

- A work surface on which papers and files can
  be spread out when they are being reviewed
- A place to store them when they aren't

In just a couple of hours, you've accomplished the first of
those needs. Within a few days, you'll find that you absolutely love it. You'll look back and wonder how you ever
got anything done when your desk was so cluttered you
couldn't even find the telephone. A clean desk is an eye-
opener—and a great motivator.

There's an extra bonus in having an organized, efficient
desk. Suppose a client of yours, John H., enters your office
for a meeting and sees on your desk only a telephone, a
pad of paper, and the file for the project that is to be discussed. Not only is he surprised, but he's intimidated. He
has never seen such a neat, organized desk, and doesn't
know what to make of it. He mumbles to himself, "Don't
you have any work to do, or are you so good that you've
completed it?" But after the meeting, he's very impressed.
You've shown that you were well prepared and had a complete grasp of the project. It was a very successful meeting.
Congratulations.

As impressive as it is, your uncluttered desk wasn't the
real reason for that successful meeting. It was your Master
List, which, for the moment, you had put in a desk drawer.

Somewhere on that list was an item like this: "Meeting with John H.—Tues. 10:00 A.M.—Discuss new project." You wrote that item on your Master List a week ago when the appointment was made, and with that as a reminder, you were well prepared for the meeting.

In fact, you've been using one simple strategy to deal with every item of unfinished business on your Master List. Each evening before you went home, you scanned your Master List from top to bottom and asked yourself, *"What is the most important thing that I must do tomorrow?"* When you arrived at the office the next morning, you did it—and had the pleasure of crossing it off your list!

Creating and Using Your Own Master Files

Making a Master List of your ongoing jobs is only the first step in creating a truly efficient work space. Once you've gone through all these piles of files and have tossed out all the papers you don't need, you have to find a place to put the ones you want to keep. You should put those papers in separate file folders.

Use File Folders

You may have developed a fear of file folders. Why? Because there's no place to put them. Your desk is stacked with papers, and the file drawers are filled beyond capacity. However, there's a good reason why you should use file folders. All the papers regarding a client, a customer, a specific project, or an item of business should be kept together. When you review this information at a later date, all the facts, reports, notes from meetings, telephone conversations, and correspondence are right there for you to study before you undertake a project or make a decision.

Too often jobs are done and decisions are made without reviewing all the relevant information that's available. This can be very expensive in both time and money. Obviously, having all the relevant materials at hand is the best way to tackle any job or solve any problem. If you get into the habit of keeping all the related papers and documents for your ongoing projects together in a file folder, you'll also take more notes on your telephone conversations and business meetings. In the past you may not have jotted down things like that, because it just created another piece of paper to deal with. But those notes can be a great aid to your memory—and now you have a place to put them. *Remember, though, never put a piece of unfinished work inside a file folder without first noting it on your Master List.* If it isn't on the list, it will be forgotten.

Collate Your File Folders

For your Master File, use folders that have tabs in three separate positions, left, center, and right. When you open the box, you'll see that the folders have *not* been collated; all those with a tab on the left are grouped together, as are those with center and right tabs. Take a few minutes to rearrange the folders so that the tabs are staggered.

You can now see three file labels at once. That may seem trivial, but when you've placed all the folders in a drawer, you'll find it much easier to locate your files. It'll save you a lot of time.

Label Your File Folders

As you go through the papers you want to keep, it should be easy to separate them into different categories: personnel, budget, expenses, customer X, project Y, etc. But don't just make new piles. Place each group of related papers in a file folder. And, of course, on each folder you will need to write a name or title that is both easy to read and quick to find.

You'll also need a generic file that is a catchall for the miscellaneous papers that must be kept for a short time. This file can be titled "Things to Do." After you've completed the work, the papers can be placed in a permanent file or tossed.

Write File Labels by Hand

In my opinion, it's a waste of time and money to type labels for your file folders. If you're going to have the label typed, you'll probably write it out on a piece of paper and hand it to your secretary, who will then type the name on a gummed label and give it back to you, one, two, or three days later. If you're going to take the time to write out the label, write it on the folder yourself, and it's done! You have the file immediately and have eliminated some work that would have kept your secretary busy instead of productive.

Write the name or title of the file directly on the tab of the folder with a ballpoint pen. Pencils smudge and look messy; felt-tip pens are sometimes so broad that they are illegible. It isn't necessary to use a gummed label. Write directly on the tab—another little way to save time and effort.

Different-colored pens or markers can help you identify frequently used files. Your handwriting may not be the most beautiful in the world, but that is not important; you're trying to be efficient and productive. The thing that has the most beauty is a bigger paycheck.

Keep a supply of file folders in your desk drawer so that they are convenient to use. Make life easy on yourself. When you need to create a new file, simply pull a new folder out of the drawer, write the label on the tab, put the papers in the folder, and put the folder inside your file drawer. The job is done in seconds.

Use New File Folders

Don't be afraid to throw away used folders that are beat up, dog-eared, and dirty. Replace them. People often spend a great deal of time and effort just to reuse a folder that only cost a nickel. They reverse it and write on the back side, or erase the old label and write a new one, or place a new gummed label over the old one—all this in the name of saving the company some money.

I've been in offices that save all their old file folders so that they can be used again. They make the office look very messy and unprofessional, and no one ever uses the folders anyway. It's a waste of space to store them and a waste of time and effort to reuse them. Does an old folder have more value than your time? Use a new one!

A file folder should *not* be used as a notepad. If you need to write something—a name or phone number—use a piece of paper, then put it *inside* the folder. Attach business cards to a piece of paper and put it inside the folder; don't staple them to the folder. If you need to attach something to the inside of the folder, use a Post-it note. That way it can be removed and reattached to a new folder when the old one gets beat up. Don't attach notes to the outside of a folder, because they may fall off.

Your file folders should look as neat and crisp as the shirt or blouse you just picked up from the dry cleaner. Go into your business meetings with folders that are brand-new. It makes a great impression.

Group Related Papers

When you have a folder that contains a lot of papers, it makes sense to group those that relate to each other using either a paper clip or a staple. Take all the papers out of the folder, decide which of them can be grouped together, then determine in what order the papers should be arranged within the folder. Papers that you refer to the most should be placed on top. Those that are used less frequently should be placed beneath.

Use Expandable File Pockets

You've now gone through all your piles of files, created a Master List of your unfinished work, and have a stack of new file folders, labeled and filled with the papers that were formerly scattered all over your desk. Are you wondering where to put the file folders? The answer is to use expandable file pockets, which will be placed inside your file drawers. File pockets come in various widths. I've found that as a rule the ones that expand to three and a half inches are the easiest and most convenient to use.

Files that you use all the time or that are important to you should be placed in the file drawer in your desk, since it's the most convenient drawer in your office. (This will be discussed next.) The rest of your files can be stored in the credenza or a filing cabinet. The files that must be kept even though you may never look at them again should be placed in permanent storage, either in the file room or at another location. There's no reason why these papers should remain in your office.

Organize Your File Folders

Separate the file folders that you will use frequently from the ones that you won't, then separate the important folders from the unimportant ones. Put all the least important folders inside one of the file pockets. When expanded, the file pockets stand up by themselves. You may then want to rearrange the order of the folders. Files that you will refer to

more often should be placed in the front of the file pocket.
Now you're ready to tackle the folders that are important or will be used frequently.

- Make separate piles for all the folders that are
  related to each other. For example, there could
  be sets of folders for the budget, personnel,
  new client presentations, accounting/financial
  information, etc.
- Take these separate groupings and put each
  into its own file pocket. Everything that is related is now stored together.
- Arrange these folders in order of importance or
  according to frequency of use (not alphabetically). They will be easier and quicker to locate.
- There will probably also be a group of frequently used folders that have nothing in common with each other. Put them in one file
  pocket; this will be your miscellaneous catchall.

Your file pockets should now be filled with file folders
neatly grouped by subject, importance, and frequency of
use. Notice that the file tabs are easy to read and locate
because they are staggered.

If you would like to make the files even easier to find,
you can color-code the tabs. Draw a line across the top of
each tab with a colored highlighter. For example, you might
make your budget files blue, personnel yellow, customers
red, etc.

These file pockets will eventually be placed inside the
file drawer of your desk. In the meantime, just to keep
them off the top of your desk, you can place them on the
credenza or even the floor.

By now you may be experiencing complete and total

shock, or feeling a great deal of insecurity because your
desk is absolutely clean and all your important papers have
been placed in file folders. These reactions are perfectly
normal. Give yourself time to become accustomed to your
clean, organized desk. You'll soon begin to enjoy it, because you now have a place to work with great efficiency.

Organize Your Master File Drawer

The next step in the process of getting organized is to tackle
the file drawer in your desk. Are you one of the many
people who fill their desk drawers with everything *except*
important files and papers? From the things I've found, you
would think some people were running a dime store, a
museum, or an antique warehouse instead of a business.
They keep shoes, Kleenex, shoe-shine kits, purses, cloth-
ing, books, umbrellas, appointment calendars going back a
decade, old magazines and newspapers—you name it.
Open your file drawer, and I'm sure you'll find more items
to add to the list. There's probably one thing missing: your
files and papers. They've been sitting in piles on your desk.

I've even visited offices where the files belonging to the
previous occupant had never been removed. They've been
there for two or three years, and no one has ever bothered
to look at them. That's one of the reasons why everything
ends up on top of the desk.

The file drawer inside your desk is the most important
drawer in your office. It's the easiest and most convenient
drawer to use. Instead of using it to store all your unimportant things, why not try a novel idea: use it to store your
important papers and files?

You may be one of the few people who actually use the
file drawer to store their working files. If so, congratulations. Nevertheless, your file drawer is probably already
filled to capacity, so that you still don't have anyplace to
put all the papers that used to be piled on your desk.

Remove Your Hanging Files

One of your problems may be hanging files. Many of today's desks are designed to use hanging files in order to
keep the file folders from falling over. Unfortunately, this
system is not very efficient; the hanging files themselves
may take up 40 percent of the space inside the drawer, even
when they are *empty*.

Hanging files also make it difficult to get your file folders in and out of the drawer. Once you place your file
folders inside the hangers, it makes the drawer even tighter
and causes several other problems:

- It may be impossible to see a file label if the
  folder sits very low in the hanger.
- If too many files are stuffed into the hanger,
  the file tabs will brush against the top of the
  drawer when it's being opened or closed, de-
  stroying the tabs and making it impossible to
  locate your files.
- If you write a label on both the file folder and
  the hanging file, you're doing the same task
  twice, wasting time and energy—being busy
  instead of productive.

When you run out of filing space, the usual solution is
to purchase another file cabinet. That incurs additional expenses: the cost of the cabinet itself as well as of the square
footage needed to store it. Moreover, when you have available space, you tend to keep papers that should have been
thrown away. Pretty soon the extra space you need for
important but infrequently used files is no longer there.

The important papers that relate directly to your unfinished work and ongoing projects, as well as the files that
you refer to frequently, belong in the file drawer in your
desk, where you can get to them easily and conveniently. If

you don't have enough space for these files, there are two simple ways to solve the problem:

- Clean out the file drawer in your desk.
- Use expandable file pockets instead of hanging file folders.

Empty Your File Drawer

It should be fairly easy to clean out your file drawer, since most of your working papers have been on your desk. The things inside your file drawers are probably history. Let's go through your file drawer, one file at a time, and decide the fate of these papers. By now the questions you must ask yourself should be familiar:

- Do I need to keep these papers?
- Will they be looked at again?
- Am I the only person in the company who has this information?
- Can I get this information from someone else if I need it?

Depending on the answers to those questions, you should either keep the files or toss them. If you decide to keep a file but its old folder is beat up, make a new one for it.

You may have an emotional attachment to a few of your files. Some of the memories will be good ones; others are best forgotten. If you find it difficult to make a decision, for whatever reason, keep the file but put it in another drawer. It's OK to defer a final decision to another day, when you're in a less sentimental mood.

Go through the papers in each file and decide if everything is still necessary. You'll probably discard many of the papers; only a few will be important enough to keep. Weeding out individual files will relieve a lot of the crowding inside the drawer.

You'll be amazed that so much junk has been lying around for so long. When you're finished, there should be only a handful of files that are "keepers," and your wastebasket should be filled to the brim. An enormous burden has been lifted off your shoulders, and you should feel great.

Now that you've placed your folders inside the expandable file pockets, you don't need the hanging files any longer. Do you want to give them to someone else, put them in storage (where they will sit forever), or throw them out? My advice is to toss them.

The next step is to organize the papers from any old files that you want to keep. Some of them can be merged with the new files you have already created. Others may require a file folder of their own. Once that job is done, place these files inside expandable file pockets, just as you did with the papers on your desk.

You now have an empty drawer, and all your important papers are in labeled file folders, which you have put inside file pockets. Place the file pockets inside your file drawer so that the folders face you when the drawer is open. It'll be much easier to read the names on the tabs and locate a file.

The proper placement of your files will also make life easier. Files that you use quite frequently should be in the front of the drawer, giving you easy access. Files you don't look at very often should be placed behind them.

With this final step, you have now created your Master File. All the important papers relating to your job are grouped together in labeled file folders that are easy to find and retrieve. The time it took to organize your Master File is minuscule compared with the time you'll save by using it.

Organize Your Other Drawers

The job isn't quite done yet. If you're like most people, you've put a lot of miscellaneous papers and personal items inside your other desk drawers and have never looked at them again. Empty the contents of each drawer onto the top of your desk. Take a few minutes and go through the pile. If there are papers you want to keep, put them inside the appropriate file folder and place them in the file drawer; if there are other things to keep, put them back into the drawer. Throw the rest of the stuff away.

Place your pens, pencils, stapler, paper clips, Scotch tape, and other office supplies in a drawer. Whenever you use them, be sure to put them back where they belong when you're finished. It isn't necessary to leave them out all the time.

If your telephone is on the credenza, move it to your desk. There's plenty of room for it now. It will make your life much safer, since you'll be able to use the phone without the risk of strangling yourself. Your mementos and other personal things can be moved to the credenza.

You've now finished a job you probably thought couldn't be done. You have moved mountains. In just the span of two or three hours, you've cleared off the piles of paper that cluttered your desk, cleaned out your desk drawers, and created a convenient, efficient filing system.

Sit back in your chair, put your feet up on your clean desk, and relax. How long has it been since you've seen such a beautiful expanse of desktop? Remember what it used to look like just a few hours ago? What's on it now? A telephone and your Master List. *That's all!* Your files have been put away, and everything else is out of sight—but easy to find—in the drawers of your desk.

In a week or two you should plan to go through the papers in your credenza and file cabinets, too. The process is exactly the same. Less frequently used files, or those you need for permanent reference, can be ordered alphabetically or by year. Files that you *never* use should be moved out of your office permanently. Once this job is done, you'll have plenty of room for the files you may ultimately want

to remove from the drawer in your desk. Now you not only
have an efficient desk, you have an efficient office.

An Efficient Desk Is Easy to Maintain

When you go through the papers that flood your office
every day, decide immediately which ones to toss and
which ones to keep. Don't backslide and begin to build new
piles all over your desk. File papers immediately in the
appropriate folder, or create a new file and put it away.
Here are some tips to help you *stay* organized:

- Always note on your Master List any unfinished work or future projects.
- *Never* put a piece of paper representing unfinished work in a folder unless you've first written it on your Master List.
- When it's time to tackle any project, just pull
  the relevant file and complete the work. When
  you're finished put it away—don't leave it on
  your desk—and enjoy the pleasure of crossing
  that item off your Master List.
- When you see a few piles accumulating, or
  when papers and files you're not using at that
  moment begin to creep across your desk, *stop
  cold and reorganize yourself*. It'll only take you
  fifteen or twenty minutes to get yourself back
  together.

Once you know how the system works and have ex-
perienced the wonderful benefits of being organized, you
won't have any difficulty staying that way. No longer will
you waste time searching through random piles of disor-
ganized files trying to locate that one important piece of
paper. You won't forget important projects, or remember
them only at the last minute. Your Master List will serve as

a continual reminder of the things you need to do, and your Master File will contain all the necessary information.

Now that you have a whole desk to use and enjoy, and a Master List and a Master File that will guarantee the most efficient use of your time and an increase in your productivity, it's time to get on with the business of the day.

Open Your Door

The first thing you'll see is a crowd of surprised, amazed, and envious faces as your colleagues pass by your office and wonder what happened. Those expressions should add to your sense of satisfaction for a job well done.

PART II

MAKE YOUR DAY
WORK FOR YOU

1

Give Yourself a Raise

Putting a higher value on your time will help you save time

You've heard the old saying "Time is money." But have you ever stopped to think what it really means? Rephrasing it makes it perfectly clear: *When you waste time, you waste money!*

We're very concerned about how we spend or invest our money. We're always searching for value. Why don't we try to maximize the worth of our time, too? The most precious asset we have is time. You're paid a salary not only for your abilities but also for the time you spend at work. You should both give and get full value for it. But time—and money—is wasted every day from the top to the bottom of every business and organization. That waste is unnecessary.

Anyone who works for himself—an independent contractor, a free-lancer—has a pretty good idea of what his time is worth, because he charges for his services by the hour. But if you're on a company payroll at an annual salary, an hour may not seem to mean much one way or another.

Why not look at it this way? Let's say you're the CEO of a major corporation, earning a salary of $500,000 annually. How much is an hour of your time worth? Figure it out: $500,000 a year for fifty-two forty-hour weeks translates into roughly $250 an hour. You can bet that the executives paid at that salary level are aware of how much every hour of their time is worth—and of how much every wasted hour costs their companies.

Why not play a little game with yourself? Whatever your present salary, imagine that you're being paid $600 an hour, or exactly $10 every minute. That means if you sit in a reception room for fifteen minutes, you've wasted $150. If a meeting drags on for an extra thirty minutes, that costs your company $300 in your salary alone—not to mention the salaries of everybody else at that meeting. Get stuck on the phone in idle conversation for ten minutes, and that's another $100 wasted. In other words, even the smallest waste of time can cost big money.

Whether you're paid $25,000, $50,000, or $100,000 a year, *think big*. Place a higher value on your time. You'll have a greater awareness of just how much a few wasted minutes can cost. You'll be motivated to eliminate wasted time and accomplish much more. In fact, it's only with that attitude and motivation that you're likely to end up earning a great deal more someday.

Of course, nobody is 100 percent efficient. We're not robots, after all. It takes time—and it's important—to get organized, to think, even to socialize. But it's just as important to save the time that is too often wasted—time you can use to become more efficient, more productive, and more valuable to your company.

In Part One, you saw how you can save at least thirty minutes every day just by having an organized and efficient desk and filing system. But time can slip through your fingers in other ways during the course of a typical business day. In the following pages, I'll show you how to save another thirty minutes or more of wasted time by practicing a few simple techniques and strategies. That's an *hour* of more productive time every day.

I can already hear you saying, "That's just great for the boss or owner of the company. What's in it for me? I'll be working twice as hard for the same salary."

First of all, you won't be working twice as hard. Your workday will be smoother and easier because you're organized. You won't be continually faced with nerve-frazzling crises; instead of creating problems, you'll have time to solve them. You'll actually begin to enjoy the parts of your job that you used to dread. You'll get results, and with results come rewards. When you work more efficiently and hence more productively, not only are you saving your company money, you're helping it make *more* money. You've increased your value to the company and are worth more. You can expect to get a raise—and probably a promotion as well.

2

Things to Do Today

Master your work with your Master List

It's easy for the day to slip away from you without your ever realizing it. The loss of time is very subtle. Interruptions, telephone calls, meetings, emergencies—all steal your valuable and precious time. As a result, you come in early, stay late, and go home without having accomplished half of what you intended to do that day.

There's an easier way. Use the Master List you created in Part One. That list is the key to an efficient and organized business day. It will tell you at a glance what ongoing projects and unfinished business should command your attention from the moment you arrive at the office in the morning to the time you leave at night.

Look at the sample Daily Agenda Sheet on page 53 and copy it on a large piece of paper. This sheet is just a planning tool to show you how to get into the habit of organizing your workday. Referring to your Master List, fill in the "Things to Do Today" column with all the important projects you plan to work on tomorrow. Include your scheduled appointments, as well as time to return phone calls and complete routine correspondence and other paperwork.

Daily Agenda Sheet

Things to Do Today	Things I Actually Did
8:00	8:00
9:00	9:00
10:00	10:00
11:00	11:00
12:00	12:00
1:00	1:00
2:00	2:00
3:00	3:00
4:00	4:00
5:00	5:00

Where Did the Day Go?

Don't worry about putting too much on your Daily Agenda Sheet. The important thing is to get an idea of just how you plan to spend your day and to get the feel of scheduling and controlling your time. You've now gone one step beyond your Master List. You've made a list of the important things you plan to do tomorrow and decided when to do them. You've created an agenda for a full day's work.

When you've completed your agenda, look it over quickly just before you leave the office for the day, to refresh your memory. If there are some papers or files you need to review for tomorrow's projects, take a few extra minutes and look at them before you leave, or if necessary tuck them in your briefcase and go over them at home.

When you arrive at the office the following day, look at your Daily Agenda Sheet before you do anything else. Then try to follow it as closely as possible. As the day goes by, fill in the "Things I Actually Did" column, detailing how you ended up spending your time.

This is a very revealing exercise because it gives you a comparison between what you planned to do that day and what you actually did. You'll now be able to see just how you spend a typical day at the office. The more specific you made your daily agenda and the more details you recorded in your diary of activities, the more information you'll have about how your time was really spent.

By comparing your agenda with your actual activities, you'll also see that going to the trouble of making an agenda for every day's work would be a waste of time. You may have put in one of the most productive days of your week, but it won't correspond to your agenda, because some unexpected project arose, or you had to deal with an unpredictable situation. Unless your job is completely routine—and most are not—it's almost impossible to predict in advance the course of any business day.

That's where your Master List comes in. It's not carved in stone. It's flexible, adaptable to any situation. You'll add new items of business as they arise throughout the day, and cross out others when the tasks are completed. Consult your Master List before you leave the office every night. If there's a major project or something that *must* be worked on the following day, note it on your calendar for that day and make an appointment with yourself to get the job done. If there are some papers or reports you need to review for the project, look at them before you leave, or take them home with you. Then, when you arrive back at the office, check your Master List, look at your calendar—and get to work.

First Things First

How to establish your priorities

Let's suppose you've noted a number of important projects on your Master List. How do you decide which project to do first? Which one gets top priority?

In most cases like this you'll *know* which project should come first. But if you have difficulty deciding between some of the others, here's a method that will help. Write your important projects in any order on a numbered list.

1. _____   4. _____

2. _____   5. _____

3. _____

Then choose between each of the items as follows, and on your list put a check mark beside your choice:

1 or 2, 1 or 3, 1 or 4, 1 or 5,
2 or 3, 2 or 4, 2 or 5,
3 or 4, 3 or 5,
4 or 5

The project that has the most check marks is the most important.

Now that you know where your priorities lie, write that project on your daily calendar and schedule a specific time to get it done.

Don't Panic

Handling emergencies

There's a world of difference between something that's "important" and something that's "urgent." A dictionary would define the words as follows:

IMPORTANT: adj., of much significance or consequence

URGENT: adj., pressing; compelling or requiring immediate action or attention; imperative

We all begin our day with every intention of getting our important work done: long-term projects, reports about operations of the company, sales presentations, plans for the future. We know they're important, but somehow we don't get to them. We're distracted, interrupted, or have to drop everything because some crisis has arisen or there's some problem that has to be solved *now*. Something *urgent* has forced its way to the top of our list of things to do, and we have to drop everything to deal with it at that very moment. *The "important" has been knocked out by the "urgent."*

There are times, of course, when an unexpected crisis or problem presents a genuine emergency. In that case, it is imperative to rise to the occasion, to keep cool and deal with it to the best of your ability. But quite often the fires that need your immediate attention are the result of arson. Something should have been done—and it wasn't. So now you have a problem, a crisis, an emergency, and you must devote your valuable time, energy, and resources to finding a solution.

It may be impossible to prevent every emergency, but when you're forced to drop everything to put out a fire, your important projects also go up in smoke. You've lost control over your own priorities. You're reacting to events instead of making them happen—following instead of leading.

Some people claim they thrive on crises and work better under pressure. They're kidding themselves. It's usually an excuse for putting off the important projects until the last minute, when they'll have no other choice. There's no time left to think, to analyze, to correct the inevitable mistakes. Even if these people seem to function well under pressure, think how much more effective they would be if they scheduled their own important projects to give themselves more time and fewer headaches.

There are three ways to be sure you'll be able to handle both the important and the urgent jobs smoothly:

- First and foremost, schedule your own major projects and complete them *before* they become urgent and you—or somebody else—has to put out the fire.
- Second, when something urgent does come up, as it inevitably will, give yourself a little time to think it through. A well thought out

solution is always better than an impulsive one.

- Third, you should anticipate that a number of unforeseen problems will pop up every day. You may not be able to predict these problems, but you can include the time to solve them in your schedule.

Again, that's the beauty of your Master List. It's flexible. You'll find that in most cases you'll be able to note the problem on your Master List, complete the project you're working on, solve the problem, then proceed to the next project on your list—without missing a beat. You'll discover a world of difference in your daily productivity if you give precedence to your important work and projects instead of responding impulsively to every urgent crisis that arises. In the long run, you'll save time and spare yourself a lot of useless anxiety—and maybe even the pain and discomfort of an ulcer.

During a business day, very little happens that's actually life-threatening and needs your immediate attention. You can probably put off tackling an unexpected problem for at least a half hour, or even a half day. Avoid the impulse to drop everything in order to put out the fire immediately. You don't need to stop what you're doing at that very moment. It's usually far more important to complete the task you're working on, and then take the time to think about and solve the unexpected problem.

5

Prime Time

Use your most productive time to do your most productive work

For most of us, the most productive time of day is the early morning. We're fresh, alert, and rested. We have lots of energy and are ready to go to work. Our level of concentration is very high and we have a long attention span. As the day progresses, we usually begin to tire and lose concentration and interest. The quality of our work slides, unless we get a second wind. If you've postponed working on your important projects until you've begun to run out of steam, both the quality of your work and your overall productivity will suffer. In other words, you're wasting your most productive hours.

It makes a great deal of sense to tackle your most difficult and important work at the time of day when you're at your best and are most likely to be able to complete it. You probably already know when you're most productive: early or late morning, early or late afternoon. Whenever it is, the objective is to keep that time for yourself—and use it efficiently.

6

The Sidetrack Syndrome

How to handle detours and trivial details

It's all too easy to get sidetracked by unimportant jobs and routine office work during your most productive hours. Consider whether any of the following applies to you:

- Do you arrive at the office first thing in the morning all set to go, but then begin to look through your "in" box or finish up a few little jobs left over from the day before?
- Do you spend your entire morning in meetings?
- Do you have morning meetings *away* from your office?
- Do you handle routine correspondence and paperwork first thing in the morning, or do other little jobs that take more time than imagination?
- Do you drop everything whenever someone

slips a piece of paper into your "in" box, or
every time there's a mail delivery?
- Do you make unimportant telephone calls?

Usually one trivial little chore leads to another, and
before you know it, the morning is gone. You've yet to
begin your most important jobs—and you've wasted your
most productive hours dealing with "administrivia."

There are two ways to lick what I call the *Sidetrack
Syndrome*. First, there's your good old reliable Master List.
Scan that list before you go home at night, decide which is
your most important project for the next day, and schedule
it on your calendar for your most productive hours. When
you get back to the office, you will have two reminders:
your Master List and your calendar. Stick to your schedule.
Don't allow yourself to be sidetracked. You'll get the job
done and save a lot of time in the process.

The second way also involves sticking to a schedule.
True, you can't ignore routine office work; you've got to
write letters and make phone calls. But why perform these
less important tasks during your most productive hours, or
scatter them throughout the day, so that you are constantly
sidetracked?

Set aside a *specific time* on your schedule for those little
jobs, after you've completed your more important projects
or perhaps between projects. Mark that time on your calendar. If someone drops something in your "in" box, ignore it. Forget the mail, the routine paperwork, and the
phone calls until *after* you've finished your most important
business and are ready to tackle the trivia. Check your Master List and pick off the little jobs one by one. Make your
phone calls, look at the mail, and handle all of the other
routine tasks that have come up since your last trivia time.
If you have a tendency to put off the minor jobs because
they're boring or time-consuming, lumping them all together will save you time, and you'll get them out of the

way. Best of all, you'll have given yourself uninterrupted, concentrated time to get your really important work done.

If you're most productive in the morning, why waste that extremely valuable time in a meeting (unless, of course, that happens to be the most important project of the day)? Routine morning meetings can knock your entire day off track. Afterward, you'll feel rushed and pressured because there won't be enough time to do the things you really wanted to do.

Why not flip-flop your day? Schedule all your routine meetings after 11:00 A.M. and give yourself the entire morning to work. The majority of your meetings probably use up more time than creative energy. Block out the morning hours for yourself and save the routine meetings for later.

It's a simple and logical approach. But if you want to keep this time for yourself, you'll have to fight for it. You may not be able to eliminate morning meetings altogether, but you can certainly try to avoid them. When you're asked to attend one, why not say that you have a conflict and offer an alternative time or day? You can usually find a more convenient time for the meeting, if you ask for it.

Whatever your most productive hours, keep them for yourself and you'll be able to shave a lot of wasted time off your workday. There's an additional benefit! If you give yourself a solid stretch of really productive time, you'll have the satisfaction of getting the job done. That will give you the momentum to get through the rest of the day with all flags flying.

7

Your Most Important Date

Schedule an appointment with yourself to get your most important jobs done

When you want something done, you usually schedule an appointment, right? You set up appointments with your doctor, your dentist, your garage mechanic; you schedule them with your boss, your customers and clients, your colleagues. An appointment is a mutual agreement to meet with someone at a specific time. You write it on your calendar. Here's a good question: If you have an important job to do, *why not schedule an appointment with yourself and write it on your calendar?* When the time comes, keep the appointment with yourself, just as you would any other, and get the job done.

Here's how it works. Consult your Master List and note which of the jobs that must be done will require a solid block of uninterrupted time. Now note the deadline, the time at which you know that the work must be completed. Flip open your calendar and make an appointment with yourself, setting aside a particular day and time specifically to do that job. It could be tomorrow or next week, depending on the deadline. Give yourself plenty of leeway—no putting it off until the last minute. Don't cross that project off your Master List after you've entered it on your calendar—you haven't got it done yet. Your Master List will serve as your daily reminder, and your calendar will pinpoint the specific day and time you intend to complete the project.

Give yourself more time than you think you'll need to finish the work. If you estimate it will take fifteen minutes, allocate a half hour; if you need an hour, give yourself two. It'll make your life much easier, less hectic, and will take the pressure off. If you don't give yourself enough time, then you'll have to stop, put the job aside, and return to it later. You may end up doing the same task twice. Quite often you'll complete the project in less time than you had anticipated. Congratulations. Now you can go on to something else.

Most of us have a tendency to underestimate the amount of time it will take to complete something that seems easy, and to overestimate how much time it will take to complete something that looks difficult. Give yourself a cushion, because as the due date gets closer and closer, the pressures and tensions will grow proportionally.

You may not always be able to keep your appointment with yourself. Something more important may come up, or you may find that you don't yet have all the necessary information. You can be flexible. Reschedule the appointment, and in the meantime collect the necessary information in the appropriate folder in your Master File. You'll find that when you make a date with yourself, it will stick in your mind. You'll start thinking about that project beforehand, and you may well come up with some imaginative new approaches or creative ideas before you even start working on the task. Knowing you have to keep that appointment will set your creative juices flowing and save you time.

There are some other timesaving benefits, too. If you

know exactly when you're going to tackle and complete a project, you can promise delivery—and *keep* that promise. You can set precise deadlines for the reports and information you'll need, because you know when you'll need them. So whether the work to be completed is an important project or a collection of trivial ones you simply want to get out of the way, schedule an appointment with yourself—and keep it!

8

No Trespassing

How to avoid interruptions

How many times have you started a project at 9:00 A.M. and found that you haven't completed it by noon? Have you ever felt like an entire day has been wasted? You've spent eight or ten hours at the office, yet you haven't accomplished anything? Hours of valuable time have been invested without any tangible results. The whole day has been wasted. Do you have any idea why this happened? *You allowed yourself to be interrupted.*

Every day valuable time is being taken from you. It's done very subtly. There's a knock on your door, someone walks in, and before you know it, fifteen to twenty minutes have been wasted in unimportant gossip. Or you agree to help someone with his work, which means you're not doing your own. Or the telephone rings. It could be a business call or it may be social, but before you hang up another half hour has disappeared.

Once you start a project, a momentum or flow begins to develop. The first time you're interrupted, it usually takes a few minutes to regain that momentum. You need to back up a little bit in order to determine where you left off. In other words, you have to cover the same ground twice. Should there be a second interruption, it'll take you even longer to get back on track and going again. After the third or fourth interruption, you probably come to the conclusion that you aren't going to get that project done anyway and say to yourself, "Let's skip it. I'll do it later." When it's time to leave the office, the whole day is gone and you have nothing to show for it.

Meeting, talking, and working with other people is a normal—and important—part of a typical office day. However, *your* work—and the peace and quiet you need to complete it—should be just as important. Your secretary, if you have one, can be your first line of defense, taking phone calls, heading off casual visitors, or scheduling appointments. If you don't have a secretary, your best line of defense is your door.

Many companies think it's advisable to have an *open-door policy*. What they end up with, though, is an *always-available policy:* You're always available to answer questions or help solve problems or just chat. No one is ever turned away. The open-door policy invites interruptions. If you're the one who's being interrupted, it can have very time-consuming consequences. You may have to come in early or stay late in order to complete your work. If you can't get your work done between 9:00 and 5:00, it's probably because you're constantly being interrupted.

Here are a number of tactful ways you can fend off interruptions, even without closing your door:

- If someone with a problem or a question walks into your office uninvited, instead of dropping everything immediately, it's OK to say, "I'm tied up at the moment. Can you come back at (suggest a specific time) and we can talk about it then?'' Schedule a meeting to get together and discuss it at a mutually convenient time.

- If part of your job involves frequent consultations with your colleagues, schedule a specific time on your calendar for those meetings. Then let it be known that you're always available, say, from 11:00 to 12:00 in the morning, or 3:30 to 4:30 in the afternoon. An open door becomes a time-saver instead of a time waster.
- When someone comes into your office uninvited, stand up to talk. If you let your visitor arrange himself comfortably in a chair, you're in for a long interruption. Better yet, you can pretend you were just on the way out, then talk with your visitor briefly in the hall.
- If your visitor has something really important to talk about, ask him to give you a few minutes, and then go to *his* office. That way you can control the length of the conversation.
- Arrange your desk and chair so that you're not in full view of casual passersby. If they have to peek around the corner to see you, they'll usually think twice about disturbing you.
- Keep your office furniture to a minimum. A comfortable chair right next to your desk is a temptation that's hard to resist.

In most companies teamwork is important. Impromptu visits and conversations are inevitable. In fact, you can sometimes avoid a more formal and time-consuming meeting with just a few informal conversations. But you should know the difference between a necessary visit and an interruption—whether it's your time or your coworkers'. If you respect their time, they'll respect yours. When all else fails, close the door.

9

Do Not Disturb

Finding privacy when you need it

You may think that closing your office door is an affront to your colleagues, a signal that you're being aloof or are up to something sinister or secret. It's not! It shows that you take your time and your job seriously. If you close your office door for just one hour a day, you'll increase your productivity and complete your important work in half the time. A closed door will give you time to think, to concentrate—without interruptions. When you open your door again, you're announcing to the world that you've got the job done and are ready to tackle whatever comes next.

It's particularly important to close your door during your appointments with yourself. You've scheduled a specific time to work on a project during the most productive hours of your workday. Why ask for interruptions, or waste the time it takes to ward off uninvited visitors tactfully? There's no better way to convey the message that, for the moment at least, you don't want to be disturbed.

If you need longer stretches of uninterrupted time, here are a few strategies you can use:

- *Disappear.* When you need quiet time to think, to ponder a problem, or to work on a difficult project, just disappear. Reserve the conference room and don't tell anybody where you are. That's a wonderful way to escape from the telephone and avoid interruptions. If you work for a large firm, look for an unused conference room on a different floor or in a different section of the building. If a conference room isn't available, an empty office is a great place to work in privacy for brief periods of time.

- *Stay home.* Another possibility is to stay home and work there when you need uninterrupted time for a big project. There won't be any phone calls, the kids will be at school, and

your spouse will be at work. There's peace and
quiet, and you can spread all your papers out
on the kitchen table and get the job done.

- *Tell everybody that you'll be out for the day, then
  come in.* If you want a very long stretch of uninterrupted time, announce that you'll be out
  of the office for a whole day. Tell as many
  people as you possibly can, so they won't try
  to reach you. You can now come to work without any fear of interruptions or phone calls.
  Instruct your secretary or receptionist to tell
  everybody that you're out, should anyone call.
  You'll be amazed at how much work you'll be
  able to complete. It's almost like coming in on
  a Saturday.

- *Don't come to the office early or stay late.* Your
  objective should always be to spend *less* time at
  the office, not more. You may impress some
  people with your devotion to your job; on the
  other hand, they may just think you're not
  well organized enough to get your work done
  during normal working hours.

Sometimes you have no choice and must put in long
days and even weekends. However, if you work extra hours
every day, it's a sign that you're not being as productive as
you could be during regular office hours. Schedule
most important projects for your most productive office
hours and protect your privacy. You'll get a lot more done
during working hours and won't have to spend the wee
hours at your desk.

10

Don't Put It Off

How to lick the procrastination habit

Procrastination is by far the biggest waster of time, no matter what your job. We're all procrastinators to one degree or another. Mark Twain offered this piece of advice: "Never put off 'til tomorrow what you can do the day after tomorrow." The trouble is that the things we put off may *never* get done. Or when we finally do get around to doing them, we're working under the pressure of a deadline, and we don't do them as well as we could have.

If you're putting in fifty or sixty hours of work each week, you probably don't consider yourself a procrastinator; you're already a dedicated contributor to your company. But let me ask you a few pointed questions:

- Do you have a tendency to leave your unpleasant projects until the last minute?
- Do you hope that if you put off tackling some problem, it will just go away, or somebody else will solve it?

- Have you ever thought to yourself that you could do a better job if you had more time?
- When you fail to get a job done on time, do you blame someone else?
- Do you set unrealistic deadlines for yourself, which almost guarantee you won't get the job done on time?
- Do you overload yourself with work, then complain that there's too much to do?
- Are you running out of excuses and alibis to explain why your projects aren't getting done on time?

If your answer to any one of these questions is yes, you're a procrastinator! If you answered yes to more than a few of them, your career may be in big trouble.

Psychologists can cite a whole battery of reasons why people procrastinate, but the number-one reason is probably fear of failure: We postpone doing something because we're afraid we won't do it right. This striving for perfection can stop you dead in your tracks, or slow you down long enough so that you probably will fail. It becomes a self-fulfilling prophecy. Your fear of failure leads to feelings of guilt because you *know* you could have done a better job if only you hadn't waited until the last minute.

Procrastination is part of human nature, and we're all human. But when it becomes a habit—a consistent pattern in the way you do your job—it can have disastrous consequences. You end up spending more time in the office, not less, because you're not using your time efficiently. Your productivity and creativity go down the drain. You're *always* working under pressure, with a very unpleasant result: You're unhappy with your job—and yourself.

Don't despair. There are a lot of techniques you can use to beat the procrastination habit:

- *Bore yourself to death.* Whenever you feel yourself being tempted to put off some unpleasant task or are reluctant to tackle an important job, pull yourself up short. *Stop! Do nothing!* Empty your head of thoughts. Stare into space. Don't even doodle or twiddle your thumbs. I guarantee that after just a few minutes of this you'll be so totally bored that you'll be eager to start any task, no matter how unpleasant or intimidating.

- *Don't be tripped up by trivia.* A frequent trick of procrastinators is to use trivial tasks as an excuse for not starting to work on the important ones. Or, conversely, sometimes the hard-core procrastinator will put off the unpleasant and the trivial tasks until the last moment, which means they never get done. You've already learned how to handle trivia. Set aside a specific time on your daily calendar to get *all* these little jobs done. Swallow your medicine in one big gulp. It'll be good for you.

- *Give yourself a reward.* Whenever you see some unpleasant task or really important project looming ahead of you, promise yourself a little bonus when you get those tasks done. For the routine jobs, plan a brief break for a cup of coffee, or take a few minutes to scan a newspaper or magazine. When you complete a big, important project, treat yourself to something special. Buy yourself something new, have a fancy dinner at your favorite restaurant, or plan a celebration with the colleagues who were part of the project. Give yourself a big pat on the back. It'll work wonders.

- *If a carrot doesn't work, try a stick.* Whenever you're tempted to put off something, sit back and ask yourself what will happen if you *never* do it. Let your imagination wander. Will you be fired? Will your boss be fired? Could the company go bankrupt? If that's the case, *everybody* will be out of a job—and it will all be *your* fault.

  That kind of guilt and doomsday thinking will help put things in their proper perspective—both the big, important projects and the trivial ones. You won't use your trivial jobs as an excuse to postpone working on your important ones. If the work you're responsible for completing is so very important, why on earth would you wait for even five minutes to get started, when so many people are depending on you? After all, if those important things don't get done, well, bad things could—and usually do—happen.

These little tips are not the last word on procrastination. However, they can help put you into the right frame of mind to tackle and complete a project. Procrastination is a habit that *can* be broken. Here's how.

Think Before You Act

Big projects that are important to your company, or those creative projects so crucial to your career, are always intimidating. You never know where to start. Chances are, if that's your problem, it probably doesn't matter where you start, just as long as you begin, even if you're just nibbling around the edges. It's like eating an apple: You can't swallow it whole, so you take a little bite first, then another and another. Pretty soon the apple is gone.

When a project is assigned to you, begin to work on it immediately. Don't wait for your lead time to vanish. Note the job on your Master List. If there's a deadline, enter it on your calendar. Start collecting the necessary information and put it in a properly labeled file folder. Let your mind circle the project as a whole, and then begin to go over all the details. What is the time frame? Are there other people who can help you? What resources will be needed? Give yourself the time to think and plan. It'll get you started on the project and will save time in the long run.

Put all your thoughts and ideas on paper. If you're at your desk, jot them down on a notepad. Talk into a tape recorder, and then transcribe the tape. If you're walking along the street and an idea flashes through your mind, write it down. If you don't have a piece of paper, use a business card. Just don't let these valuable ideas slip away. If you write them down, then you won't need to remember them.

If you see a relevant article in a newspaper or magazine, cut it out. Start gathering pertinent information from your colleagues. Date every piece of paper you handle. That way you can see the sequence of your thoughts, and the way the project is evolving. Place all the papers you want to keep inside the file folder, and put the folder inside your file drawer, where it will be easy to find when you need it. Every few days, look through the file and review the material you've collected. It'll refresh your memory and stimulate new thoughts and ideas. Write them down, too. The more time you give yourself to think, the easier the project becomes, and the faster you'll be able to complete it.

At this point, all you're trying to do is collect ideas and information as you begin to formulate a framework for the project. It will help you develop an overview of what needs to be done and determine the direction you want to take. Now the project will seem far less intimidating, and you don't have to worry about the procrastination problem— you've already begun.

One Step at a Time Saves Time

If you're faced with a big project, why not break it down into smaller components and tackle them one by one? You'll have the satisfaction of getting part of the job done, and be that much closer to finishing the whole assignment.

Taking the time to outline a project and all its components is another big step toward getting the job done. It will also help you organize your thoughts and the sequence in which you plan to complete the work. You should review the outline frequently, and will probably rewrite it more than once as you get into the project. Each time you look at it, you'll see things a bit more clearly and your focus will become more defined.

Before you begin to do any work, take a red pen and write in the margin of your outline the length of time you think it will take to accomplish each portion of the project. Some tasks could take you fifteen or twenty minutes; others may require an hour or more. Your estimate doesn't have to be exact. Then add up the total amount of time you think will be needed to complete the work. Now you have an idea of how long it'll take to finish the job. Just to be safe, you may want to increase the figure by 50 percent. That way you'll have a cushion if you run into problems.

If it's a four-hour project, will you do it in one sitting, or spend an hour a day for four days? What if it's a twenty-hour job? Will you have to do the entire thing by yourself, or are there people available to assist you? Delegating smaller parts of a project to the appropriate person can be a big time-saver. Don't fall into the ''I'm the only one who can do this job'' trap. You'll be tempted to feel sorry for yourself—and procrastinate. If you need help, ask for it.

If you follow these small steps, it'll be easier for you to get motivated and start your work. There won't be any procrastination or inertia to overcome. By doing a little bit at a time, you'll develop the momentum to complete even the biggest of jobs. Remember, even a journey of a thousand miles begins with a single step forward.

Getting the Job Done

Once you've taken the time to organize your thoughts, write an outline, and gather the help and information you'll need, you can proceed to the next step, which should sound familiar to you. Look at your calendar, determine how much time will be necessary, and decide when you'll start on the project. Make an appointment with yourself and write it down. The night before, review the file and think about all the information you've accumulated, so that everything is fresh in your mind. When you arrive at the office in the morning, you'll be ready to get to work. Remember to schedule your important projects for your most productive time—and stay clear of sidetracks and interruptions.

Don't be paralyzed by perfectionism. No piece of work is perfect the first time through. Put your ideas and proposals in rough draft, then leave plenty of room to rewrite, edit, and refine your thoughts. That's what the creative process is all about. In most cases there's room for improvement even in the best of projects, but they are still perfectly satisfactory just as they are. Time spent trying to make something "perfect" is time wasted.

By starting early, getting organized, and taking it one step at a time, you have eased yourself into that important project, and it won't be nearly as difficult or time-consuming as you may have feared. Look at it this way: The time you spend thinking and getting organized will virtually eliminate all the time you *used* to spend worrying about the upcoming project. The hours you used to waste procrastinating have become *extra* hours that you can use creatively and productively.

11

Mark It "Urgent"

Setting deadlines for yourself

Quite often you'll let little jobs just sit on top of your desk, and they remain undone because there's no sense of urgency, no pressing need to complete them, or no specific due date. They don't appear to be very important, so you put them aside, even though they may take no longer than a few minutes to complete. There's no rush, so why do them? The problem arises when these small projects begin to accumulate and back up on you. Ultimately, the day comes when the work is needed and it still hasn't been done. Then there's a rush to complete it or a crisis to deal with.

Once you've grown accustomed to keeping track of all your unfinished projects on your Master List, you'll discover these little "no deadline" jobs have a habit of hanging around day after day, on one page after another. Projects with deadlines get done, unless you're a hopeless procrastinator and save them until the last minute. Tasks without deadlines are an open invitation to procrastinate.

We've already talked about the ways to tackle the big projects and avoid procrastination and last-minute panic. I have another technique I use to get the little jobs done—and save time in the process.

The Bogus Birthday

My best friend's birthday is October 20th. Every year I used to write it on my calendar and then just watch as the date came closer and closer, until finally I rushed out to buy a gift and, invariably, an apology card for being late. Then one day it occurred to me, why not make *October 18th* my friend's birthday? That way I could go through my usual routine, waiting until the last minute to buy a present, and it would *still* get there on time. It worked like a charm.

Try the bogus-birthday technique on those "no deadline" jobs. Make up a due date, note it on your Master List, and write it in your calendar. Even an artificial deadline creates a sense of urgency. Then if you wait until the last minute, you'll still get the little jobs done—on time—because the last minute is really the next-to-last minute.

The Squeaky Wheel Gets Greased

Use the same technique when you ask someone to do some work or obtain information for you. Create a sense of urgency; set an early deadline. If you don't, it won't get done until you've asked for it once or twice, and by then it may be too late.

Here's the way the technique works. Let's say you need a particular report for a 3:00 P.M. meeting on Friday. What's the deadline for completion that you give to the person who will prepare the report? Friday at 3:00? If so, you're asking for trouble. Why cut things so tight? Why not include a cushion, or margin for error? If you need information for a Friday meeting, insist that it be ready by

Wednesday. That'll give you a few days to think about it, absorb it, and perhaps make changes. Should the work be completed late, there's still an extra day or two.

As a general rule, ask for something a few days before it's needed and you'll eliminate a lot of pressure and tension. You may want to ask the person, "When do you think you can complete this report?" Let him set his own deadline, and hold him to it. If he isn't being realistic, suggest he give himself more time—without cutting into your own deadline.

There's an old saying: "The squeaky wheel gets greased." Be a "squeaky wheel" when it comes to reminding others about deadlines that you've set for them or that they've set for themselves. This, too, will create a sense of urgency, a feeling that the job is too important to be left until the last minute.

When it comes to your own job, your Master List will serve as that "squeaky wheel," reminding you day after day that something is still undone. If there's a deadline, move it up a couple of days to make it seem urgent—the bogus-birthday technique. If there's no deadline, make one up. Grease the squeaky wheel, and you'll find that your whole day will run more smoothly and efficiently.

12

Addition by Subtraction

*Emphasizing the important, eliminating
the unimportant*

In the early '80s, the watchword was *delegate*. The so-called secret of success was to give your job to someone else. The concept was "I'm too important to do this work myself, so I want you to do it." As a result, American business created layers upon layers of management in a corporate structure that was cumbersome, expensive, and inefficient.

Things changed toward the end of the decade. Along came foreign competition and corporate raiders. The system was forced to change overnight. All of a sudden those layers of inefficient "middle" managers were on their way out. In order to compete successfully or avoid a hostile takeover, top management had to restructure the companies. Many employees were laid off or encouraged to take early retirement. Those who were left had to do the work that in the past had been done by several people.

Today the watchword is *eliminate*. With fewer people in the company, it isn't possible to give your work to someone else. You must do it yourself or eliminate it.

Take a look at your Master List. If you're like most people, there are probably quite a few tasks on that list that shouldn't be there. Why? Here are a few reasons. Do any of them apply to you?

- Your boss gave the work to you because he didn't want to do it.
- It's not your work to do, but you're reluctant to tell your boss.
- You volunteered for this project out of the kindness of your heart, because somebody has to do it.
- A colleague asked you to help him with his work.
- Nobody else could possibly do this project as well as you can.
- You feel uncomfortable delegating jobs to other people.

You'll save yourself a lot of time by eliminating the jobs that don't belong to you. The process is called *Addition by Subtraction*. You'll add to your productive time by subtracting the busywork.

Don't Get Indigestion

Imagine yourself at a dessert table. Everything looks beautiful and delicious. There are lots of cakes, pies, tarts, eclairs, cookies, and ice cream to choose from. You want to eat them all. So you pile your plate with these wonderful delights, go back to your table, and start to eat them. By the time you've finished stuffing yourself—*if* you finish them—you feel sick. Your eyes are bigger than your stomach.

Do you do the same thing at the office? Do you say yes to every request to do additional work or take on another project, without giving any consideration to the unfinished work you're already committed to? Do you do this because you think it'll help your career? Impress your boss? Make you a martyr? If so, you're greatly mistaken. It really has the opposite effect. The truth is you'll never get everything done. You'll come in early, stay late, and never catch up. Your plate is piled so high and you're trying to eat so fast, you're going to end up with indigestion.

Learn to Say No

Be more realistic about how much work you can take on. Be honest with yourself about the length of time it'll actually take to complete a project and about the number of projects you can handle at any one time. If it's really not your job, there are tactful ways of saying so, just as there are tactful ways of delegating the work to someone else.

You don't want to get a reputation for being uncooperative or a buck passer, but if you're honest with yourself about the limitations on your time, you can be honest with everyone else. They'll respect you for it. It's far better to refuse a job than to accept it and never get it done. Keep your focus on the most important aspects of your own job. At this dinner party, that's the main course. When you're sure you can finish what's on your plate, then you can go back for seconds and think about dessert.

The Priority Payoff Formula

Suppose you do eliminate all the unnecessary jobs, and your backlog of unfinished work still looks like a seven-course meal. Do you taste a little bit of everything, yet never get it all done? If so, your priorities may be somewhat askew.

Take a long look at your Master List. Where do all of these unfinished tasks and projects fall on your priority list? Think about each item and ask yourself, "Do I *really* need

to do this?'' There's an interesting way to find out. I call it the priority payoff formula. Here's the way it works:

Give each item on your Master List a numerical value based on its *level of importance:*

1. This work must be done, and must be done well. It's a big part of my job.
2. This work is necessary, but the company's future doesn't depend on it.
3. Nobody really cares how or when I do this job.

Now give each item on your Master List a numerical value based on the *amount of time* you think you'll need to complete the work:

1. This demands a major investment of my time.
2. This requires a modest investment of my time.
3. I could do this job with my hands tied behind my back.

Now study both ratings for each item. They should be the same. In other words, the projects you rated number 1 in importance should also be rated number 1 in the amount of time you have to commit to them. If they're not, you're not using your time as efficiently and productively as you should.

If a number 1 project requires only a number 3 time commitment, for example, something is seriously wrong. For most people, however, it's the number 1's and 2's that are out of balance. Projects rated number 2 in importance are often number 1 in time commitment, while projects rated number 1 in importance don't receive enough time and attention.

Take another look at your Master List. Any project rated 1-1 is top priority, because it has the greatest payoff for both your career and your company. It obviously deserves the major share of your time and energy. The 2-2 projects have a lesser priority, because the payoff is less, but they still must be done. As for the 3-3's, there's little or no payoff, and you should try to eliminate them completely, or delegate them to someone else when possible.

What about the jobs you have rated 1-2 or 2-1? Clearly, you should begin to rethink your priorities. If you're spending the majority of your time on projects with a minimum payoff, your career is dead in the water. You're cheating yourself and your company. You're wasting your valuable skills, talents, and time on work and projects that are of marginal value. You're busy, not productive. You're certainly capable of doing more challenging and demanding work. Reverse those priorities. If your major time commitment is to those jobs with the greatest payoff, you'll be more valuable to your company, and you'll be rewarded with raises and promotions.

It's not always that easy to find the time for the 1-1 priority jobs. They're usually the big, ongoing, truly demanding projects. Somehow you must fit them in and around the necessary but less demanding 2-2 priority projects. That's why it's imperative to *save* time on the jobs of lesser importance.

Here's where the Addition by Subtraction strategy comes to your rescue. Don't overfill your plate and take on more jobs than you can reasonably handle. Try to eliminate as much of your unnecessary work as possible, then complete the jobs with only a minimum payoff as quickly and efficiently as you can. Now you'll have more time to spend on the projects that are truly important and that have the biggest payoff, both to you and your company. Now you're being productive.

13

Don't Do It All Yourself

The art of delegating

One of the best ways to get more time for those top-priority projects is by delegating some of the lower-priority work to someone else. But many people are reluctant or afraid to delegate some of their work. Do any of these reasons sound familiar to you?

- Nobody can do this work as well as I can.
- If I delegate this work, there's no guarantee that it'll get done properly.
- If someone else does this better than I do, I'm in trouble.
- I haven't got time to teach someone else how to do it.
- I want to be seen as a nice guy, not a slave driver.

You're Part of a Team

Some people won't delegate any of their work, and there are others who delegate it all. Most of us fall somewhere in between. When we try to help each other out, it's called teamwork. In a well-run organization, everyone works together as a team. Different jobs are performed by different members, and there are various levels of authority and responsibility. But the team was formed for one purpose: to get the job done successfully and help everybody go home a winner.

Think of yourself as a member of a team and you'll have a lot less trouble with the concept of delegating. Your attitude toward delegation is an important factor in asking for and getting the help and cooperation you need from the other members of your particular team.

If you delegate *only* the boring and trivial tasks to others, naturally they'll be resentful. If you toss a pile of papers on somebody's desk and say, "I want this done by Monday," that can be grounds for mutiny. Or how about the boss who gives his assistant a project and then hovers over him, checking up every five minutes to make sure it's being done to his satisfaction? Or the boss who assumes his assistant can do an unfamiliar job without any help or direction?

Here are some tips about how to approach the business of delegating that will save your time and get you the help you need:

- Ask for help, don't demand.
- Make sure the person has a clear picture of the purpose of any delegated work and knows what kind of results you expect. Take the time to talk it through, explaining specifically what you're looking for, and encourage questions.
- Give the person all the information and other

resources he'll need to complete the project.

- Set a realistic deadline that's agreeable and workable for both of you.
- Keep yourself available for questions, and when necessary ask for periodic progress reports.
- Don't assume a person will be able to complete a delegated task without any additional help or assistance from you.
- Even trivial and boring tasks are important to the smooth functioning of any team. When you do delegate them, make it clear that even though they're boring, they're necessary, and you're very grateful for the help.
- Never give a person a task you yourself aren't familiar with.
- Give the person the opportunity to use his own imagination and initiative. He may come up with some exciting new ideas.
- Never give a person a job you're not confident he'll be able to handle.
- If you feel the job is being done poorly or incorrectly, pitch in and help. Take the time to teach the person how to do it the correct way. That's what teamwork—and job training—is all about.
- When the project has been completed, give lots of praise and credit for a job well done.

Keep Track of the Work

Delegating a job to someone else doesn't mean you can forget about it. It was your job in the first place, so it's your responsibility to make sure it gets done. Put the initials of the person who's doing the work next to the item on your Master List and enter the deadline you've both agreed upon on your calendar. Don't cross that job off your Master List until it's been successfully completed; that way you will have a reminder to check up on the progress of the work, if necessary.

If you're delegating a part of a larger project, you need to make doubly sure that the work is completed on time; otherwise the whole project may be delayed. If you're the person to whom the work has been delegated, you should keep track of the dates and deadlines in the same manner.

Delegating is a confidence builder, for both the delegatee and the delegator. With practice you'll gain confidence in your own ability to delegate and in your colleague's ability to complete the work. Your colleague will become more sure of himself and of his ability to handle the job. And you will both feel the satisfaction of making an important contribution to your team—and to the success of your company.

The ability to delegate effectively has a double payoff. You'll save time, which you can spend on other important projects, and you'll send a signal to your colleagues and superiors that you're an effective manager of your time and an excellent team player—maybe even captain material.

14

Who's Minding the Store?

*How to make your meetings shorter
and more productive*

Meetings are notorious time wasters. Not only can they cut into your most productive hours, they can also sap your energy and enthusiasm and throw your entire day off schedule. But for some strange reason, meetings are a kind of status symbol, even a badge of honor. The more meetings you attend, the more important you are—or so it's thought. In fact, almost every meeting is too long, and a lot of them shouldn't be held at all.

Routine Meetings Are the Worst Offenders

Any meeting that's held just because "we always have a Monday morning meeting" becomes little more than a social gathering, with people sitting around trying to think of a reason why they're there, instead of doing more-productive work.

Impromptu Meetings Are Big Time Wasters, Too

When an impromptu meeting is called, everyone is expected to drop whatever he's doing and attend. Unless there's a real crisis, this is a terrible way to run a business. You're forced to interrupt your work flow and disrupt your schedule. You aren't prepared for the meeting and may not have the slightest idea of what's expected of you. Before you know it, an hour has been wasted without any tangible results. By the time you get back to your office, the flow and momentum that had developed earlier are gone. You may even be forced to restart your project from the beginning because you're unable to regain your lost momentum. In the long run, the quality of your work isn't as good as it could have been, the amount of work you're able to complete has been reduced, and you're probably spending more time at the office than you need to. Your career is being sabotaged.

Almost all impromptu meetings can be scheduled for later in the day or even for the next day. It's usually counterproductive to make people stop what they're doing and rush to a meeting. It's much better to have some advance warning about its purpose. Then you'll have at least a brief period of time to think about the problem and gather the necessary reports and information, so that you'll be prepared to participate effectively. As always, a considered and thoughtful response in any crisis situation is better than impulsive actions. As a rule, the only decision that's reached at an impromptu meeting is the decision to schedule another meeting—when everyone will be better prepared to discuss and handle the situation.

A Morning Meeting Can Ruin the Rest of Your Day

A morning meeting—particularly on a Monday—can slow down the momentum of the entire day or even of the whole week. Staff or sales meetings are often held first thing Monday morning, with the ostensible purpose of determining what should be done during the coming week. But if you wait until Monday to make those decisions, it's already too late. The race has started; everyone else is off and running, and you're still planning.

Monday morning staff and sales meetings can take the life, heart, and enthusiasm out of the organization. If the meeting ends after 11:00 A.M., the entire morning may be wasted. Everybody will kill time until they go to lunch. This isn't a very productive way to start a week. Furthermore, morning is the most productive time of day for many people. That's when they should be doing their work, not sitting around talking about it.

Schedule these sessions for Thursday afternoon, or Friday morning at the latest. Perhaps Wednesday afternoon would even be appropriate. By moving the meetings back a few days, you can discuss what has taken place so far that week and will still have the opportunity to do something about it, if necessary. You can also begin to plan out the coming week by discussing upcoming projects, scheduling your appointments, or anticipating your work or travel schedule.

Friday Afternoon Meetings Are Usually a Disaster, for Obvious Reasons

But afternoon meetings on any other day can pay off with a number of dividends. First and foremost, you have your mornings clear, giving you uninterrupted time to do your most productive work. You also have time to prepare for the afternoon meetings, and the momentum and motivation that develop during your productive mornings will continue and help you to be at your very best at a time when you may otherwise begin to slow down. A successful afternoon meeting will put a cap on your successful day and give you a feeling of accomplishment for that day's work.

You may not have much if any say in when your meetings are held, but you can at least discuss the problem with the people who do schedule them. They may be receptive to the idea of rescheduling morning meetings. If the time can't be changed, you may wish to come to the office an hour earlier that day, just so you can get some productive work done before the meeting begins.

If you do have some say, pay attention to both the day of the week and the time of day you choose for your meetings. This awareness will save you time, improve your productivity, and make you more valuable to your company.

Meetings are an unavoidable fact of everyday business life. But as important as they are, they're always time-consuming. If no clear course of action results or decisions aren't made, they're a complete waste of everybody's time.

Scores of books have been written about how to get the most out of a meeting. My approach boils down to two essentials:

1. If you think a meeting will be a waste of your time, don't go.
2. If you must go, make sure the meeting *won't* be a waste of your time.

Here are the most important things to consider about every meeting you attend.

Do I Really Have to Be There?

You probably don't have to go to every meeting you're asked to attend. If you don't think your presence is necessary, and if the meeting would disrupt your schedule or interfere with your productive work time, there are many tactful ways of saying no.

- Suggest that someone else attend in your place.
- Propose an alternative. Perhaps some informal conversations or a few phone calls would serve the same purpose as the meeting and save everybody time.
- If the time is inconvenient for you, ask that the meeting be rescheduled.

In the end, you may be forced to attend a meeting you feel is a waste of time, but at least you tried to avoid it.

Why Is This Meeting Being Held?

Most meetings run on too long because they have no clear-cut purpose. If everyone knew in advance what issues were to be discussed or what decisions needed to be made, the length of the meeting could be cut in half.

Whenever you're asked to attend a meeting, ask a few simple questions: "What's the purpose of this meeting? Why have I been asked to attend? Who else will be there? What will be expected of me?"

A meeting without a specific agenda is a time waster. Try to get a written outline in advance. If you're the one calling the meeting, prepare the agenda and circulate it among the participants well in advance.

Keep the agenda short. Too much on an agenda is worse than having no agenda at all. Nobody should be expected to discuss scores of different issues in one sitting. Keep the agenda short and sweet and the meeting will be short, sweet, and *successful.*

Are You Prepared?

Lack of preparation is another time waster. When you know the purpose of the meeting and what will be expected of you, write it on your Master List. Enter the time of the meeting on your calendar, make up a folder to store all the information you'll need (if you don't have one already), and keep it in your Master File.

If you're expected to speak or make a presentation, prepare your remarks well in advance. The time you take to prepare thoroughly for all your meetings will save you and everyone else at least that much time during the meeting—and probably more.

How to Keep Meetings On Time and On Track

- Expect meetings to begin and end on time. These times should be stated on the agenda. It's up to the leader of the meeting to keep to that schedule.
- Conference and meeting rooms shouldn't be too comfortable. The clock is the most important piece of furniture in the room.
- Don't wait for latecomers to arrive; start without them. When they see that the meeting has already begun, they'll get the point and be on time for the next one.
- Make the last person to arrive take the minutes.
- There should be a time limit set for the discussion of individual topics and for how long everyone is allowed to speak. This should be spelled out on the agenda. You can do your part to make a meeting run on time by being prepared and by expressing yourself within the allotted time.
- If the participants are asked to stand when it's their turn to speak, they'll be quick and to the point.
- It's up to the leader to keep every meeting on

schedule. As a participant, you can help by
avoiding unnecessary digressions and interruptions.

- If your participation isn't required for the entire meeting, why not plan to arrive at a pre-
  determined time, take part in the discussion
  that pertains to your responsibilities, and then
  leave?
- When the scheduled time for the conclusion of
  the meeting arrives, it should be announced,
  even though the meeting may continue a few
  minutes longer.

Take Notes

Even though the minutes of a meeting may be taken and
circulated later, your own notes will serve as a good reminder of what was discussed, particularly concerning
those items of business that are important to you. For easy
reference, keep your meeting notes in the appropriate file
folder and store them in your Master File; when you receive the minutes of the meeting, add them to the file.

What Was Accomplished?

One way to determine what was accomplished is to com-
pare the written agenda with the minutes of the meeting
and your own notes. Did you come away from the meeting
with a clear notion of what was achieved and what you're
expected to do as a result of the decisions that were made,
and how they pertain specifically to you and your job?
Again, your notes will serve as a reminder.

Efficient Follow-Up and Follow-Through

- New jobs or projects that you are responsible
  for completing should be noted immediately
  on your Master List.

- The dates and deadlines of new projects should be written on your calendar, along with bogus-birthday reminders, planted days or weeks ahead of the actual due date.
- The progress of ongoing projects should be updated on both your Master List and in your files. Any new deadlines should be entered on your calendar.
- Any work assigned to others that has a direct bearing on you or your projects should be noted on your Master List. Write down to whom the jobs were assigned, as well as the deadlines that were set. That way you have both a reminder and a means for follow-up.

If meetings are a major part of your workweek, it's important that you carefully schedule *your* time, as well as the times of your various appointments. A meeting that starts promptly can be a waste of time if for some reason you aren't there. Here are some tips to keep *yourself* on schedule.

The Fifteen-Minute Hedge

A famous football coach had a very simple rule: Everybody was expected to be present at team meetings *fifteen minutes* before the scheduled time. That meant the players had to arrive for a 1:00 P.M. meeting at 12:45 P.M. Use this concept when you've scheduled any meeting or appointment. Give yourself a cushion and take the pressure off. Plan to be at all your meetings fifteen minutes early. Then you can take that last-minute phone call and you'll still be on time.

Set your watch five or ten minutes fast. That way you'll have a few extra minutes before you run late. The fifteen-minute hedge is a great way to stay on schedule, not only for meetings, but throughout your workday.

Breathing Room

You can never be sure just when a meeting will end. So give yourself a little time cushion between your meetings and appointments. Don't schedule them too close together. If you run late for one, you'll be running late for the rest of the day. Should the meeting end on time or early, you're ahead of the game.

Confirm Your Meetings

When you have a meeting, it's always a good idea to re-confirm the time and place *before* you leave. You'll save yourself a lot of time—and embarrassment—if for some reason the meeting's been canceled and no one has been able to reach you.

If You're Running Late, Call First

Always leave plenty of time to get to your meetings, even those that are just down the hall. If you find yourself running late, pick up the phone and call. It's a considerate gesture on your part to let the people you're meeting with know that you won't be on time. It isn't a crime to be late. It *is* a crime when you don't call to say so.

If you don't pick up the phone, you may find—too late—that the people you're meeting with have other things scheduled and won't have enough time for you. Under those circumstances, reschedule the meeting. That way you won't disrupt the remainder of their day or yours.

How you conduct a meeting and how you conduct yourself at a meeting are two important measures of just how well you're doing your job and how valuable you are to your company. You may be able to waste valuable time in your office, and nobody will be the wiser if you somehow get your job done. But when you call unnecessary meetings, or waste time at those you're asked to attend by being late or unprepared or inefficient in your follow-up, *everybody* will be the wiser. On the other hand, if you spend time efficiently and productively—before, during, and after meetings—you're saving both your own time and the time of others. That's what they'll really notice.

15

Wheeling, Dealing, and Mealing

Getting the most out of your mealtime meetings

I never used to like meetings at mealtimes. But with today's hectic schedules and huge work loads, it can often be a productive use of your time to combine the two. Mealtime meetings essentially have two purposes aside from just breaking bread: to discuss business and to socialize and further a business relationship. The purpose you think is more important should determine which meal you choose.

Breakfast Meetings

These have become very popular lately. The so-called power breakfast has replaced the three-martini lunch as a status symbol—and that's definitely a step in the right direction. There are a number of good reasons to have breakfast meetings:

- You're fresh and wide awake.
- The menu is simple, the service is quick, and

there is no temptation to drink anything stronger than a cup of coffee.
- Everyone has someplace else to be when the normal workday begins, so breakfast meetings are usually short and to the point.

Suggest a breakfast meeting if your purpose is primarily to talk business. They are particularly useful when you or the person you want to meet with have crowded office schedules. Here's another suggestion: Hold a breakfast meeting in your own office, or in the office of the person you want to meet with. Order in coffee and Danish, and you'll save both time and money.

Luncheon Meetings

Lunch takes more time than a breakfast meeting, and you have to be careful of what you eat and drink. A heavy meal can make you sleepy for the rest of the afternoon. But luncheon meetings can serve a useful business purpose as well as give you the opportunity to socialize. Here are some pointers to get the most out of your luncheon meetings:

- Choose a restaurant you know well, where the food is good, the service is quick, and the atmosphere is quiet.
- Make sure the restaurant is convenient to everyone who's attending.
- Make a reservation for an early lunch. The best time is usually about 11:45, when there won't be any wait, the service will be good, and you'll be out quickly.
- If the meeting is primarily social, you can plan a later lunch, when the waiters won't rush you and be in a hurry to turn the table.

- Don't drink if you're going to talk business.
  And eat sensibly. You'll stay alert for the rest of
  the afternoon and add hours of productive
  time to your week.

Dinner Meetings

These rank the highest in time, money, and the temptation
to overindulge. They're useful primarily for social purposes,
when you want to "wine and dine" an important client.
Very few big deals are ever closed over dinner, but you can
start early, finish early, and make sure to set a specific date
for an office appointment or another, less social meeting at
which you *can* talk business.

There are a number of other ways you can combine
eating with meeting. Again, your choice will depend on
whether the goal of the meeting is primarily business or
social. Here are some more suggestions.

Set Up a Night on the Town

If you really want to make a fabulous impression on a
business client, try this: Invite your client and spouse to be
your guests at the restaurant of their choice and get them
tickets to a concert, a sports event, or a show. Then let them
have a romantic dinner and a night on the town—alone.
You arrange to pay for the whole evening, but stay home.
It may be the most productive dinner meeting you never
had.

Meet for a Cup of Coffee

A cup of coffee may be a good compromise for a luncheon
meeting. It feels good to take a break and get out of the
office for a little while. There's an escape from the phones

and interruptions, the restaurant is empty, and you can talk business.

Order In

If you're lunching with colleagues or coworkers, why go to a restaurant at all? Order in and sit around a desk or conference table. That's a major saving of both time and money.

Split the Check

Lunch can be a good way to get to know someone you've been working with but haven't had the opportunity to talk to about anything other than business. The atmosphere is relaxed, and you both can escape from the telephone and the office. Lunch with a colleague also offers an opportunity to do some thinking and planning, and to discuss ideas you've been playing with but haven't had the time to talk about at the office. A casual lunch with a colleague can even be more productive than your regular office meetings. Lunch with your secretary or others who help you with your job can also serve the same purpose. Or you can invite them to lunch as a reward for a job well done.

Consider Your Guest

Meeting for lunch should be the best use of everybody's time. If you sense a reluctance on someone's part to have a lunchtime meeting, it may be because he feels his time could be put to much better use. If that's the case, perhaps he'll accept an invitation for breakfast, or you might suggest that you come to his office for a brief meeting there.

When You're the Guest

The same considerations should be taken into account when you're invited to have a meal with a business acquaintance. Do you want to get to know this person better? Or would it be a better use of your time to have a meeting in your office? Suggest the time and place for the meeting that's the most suited to your purposes.

Beware the Freeloader

There's another side to this coin. There are people who won't schedule a formal business meeting, but insist on meeting you for lunch. They're probably not interested in doing business with you, but are happy to let you buy them a meal. If they don't think their time is valuable, why should you waste yours? Remember, you're not in the business of buying people meals, you're in business to do business.

Serious Business Meetings

If you want to conduct a serious business meeting, have it in the privacy of an office. There's no privacy in a restaurant, and there are constant interruptions from the waiters and busboys. Furthermore, you'll waste a lot of time on small talk instead of getting down to business. If you want to talk serious business, have your meeting first and then go out to lunch.

One Final Word

With today's prices, a lunch or dinner meeting at a nice restaurant is expensive; at a fancy one the cost can be staggering. Add in the value of the time of your guests and you're talking a major expense, particularly if you dawdle over dessert and coffee. In short, make sure your mealtime meetings achieve the results you're looking for in furthering your business relationships and social contacts or improving your business. Look for a positive payoff in both time and money *before* you sign that huge check. And always remember the three C's: your calories, the cost, and the clock.

16

Sorry, Wrong Number

Timesaving telephone tactics

The telephone is a miraculous invention and a great time-saver. It can also be a major time waster and a source of great frustration, depending on how well you use it. No matter how much time you spend on the phone, there are many ways you can improve your ability to exchange information, save time, and reduce your frustration level to zero.

No More Telephone Tag

We're all plagued by the problem of missed telephone calls. Some people call it playing telephone tag; others refer to it as trading pink slips. The game is played this way: You call someone and leave a message, he returns your call and leaves a message, and you both repeat the process over and over. When you finally reach the other party and explain the purpose of your call, he says, "Let me pull the file and call you back." The cycle begins all over again, you still don't have the information you need, and both of you have wasted a lot of valuable time.

The root of the problem is that we're all very busy. If we aren't in meetings, we're out of the office or on the phone. The odds of picking up the phone and reaching another person on the first call are less than one in five, or 20 percent.

The problem is magnified if the call is more important to one of the parties than to the other. For example, when you leave a message asking someone to return your call, you may not be the highest priority on his return-call list. You may not even be on the list. The call is important to you but not to him, and may not be returned.

Remember, even if your call is returned, there's less than a 20 percent chance that you'll be available to answer it. If you are available when the phone rings, you've been interrupted from whatever work you were doing. Every time you leave a message for someone to return your call, you're inviting an interruption. There's a better way to overcome these odds.

Don't Wait for a Return Call—Call Back Later

If you need to reach someone, call him over and over until you actually speak to him. That may sound like a waste of time, but it won't be if you give the person who answers your call your name and say that you will call back. Then proceed as follows:

- Try to find out when the person you want to speak to will be available to take your call.
- Explain the purpose or nature of your call so that the person you're trying to reach will have the necessary file or information available when you call back.

- Ask the person who's taking your message to try to find the information you need so that it will be available when you call back.
- Always ask to have your message read back to you just to make sure that it was written down, and written correctly.
- If you do want your call to be returned, your message should include the time when you'll be available to receive the call. That way you can minimize interruptions of your time.

In other words, don't just leave a message asking someone to call you back. He may not, or if he does he may not know the reason for your call. Your message should always include:

- Your name and number
- The reason for your call
- When you'll call back, or the best time to return your call

The odds of your getting through the next time will greatly improve.

Nothing is more frustrating than waiting around for someone to return a call. Many of the files and papers that clutter your desk are there because someone is supposed to call back. Take the initiative. Assume that no one will return a telephone call. Leave a detailed message—and call back.

When to Call—When to Answer

A telephone call is an interruption only if you *allow* it to be an interruption. That's true whether you're making the call yourself or someone is calling you. There are two general guidelines to follow when you're the caller:

- Set aside a specific time in your schedule to make necessary calls. That way you won't be continually interrupting *yourself* whenever the impulse strikes you to pick up the phone.
- Try to make any call at a time when the person you want to reach is most likely to be there to receive it. If you don't know what time that is, try to find out.

These guidelines may sound contradictory, but they're really not. Both involve a definite schedule for your calls, which can be written on your Master List and your daily calendar. A few minutes of preplanning your telephone calls will save you many more minutes in the long run— just like everything else you do throughout your workday.

What about when someone's calling you? Here you need to make a quick decision: Whose time is more valuable, yours or the caller's? If yours is more important, don't take the call. If the caller or the call itself is more important, take it.

For example, if you've scheduled an appointment for a period of uninterrupted time in order to complete some important work, ask your secretary, assistant, or receptionist to take messages and tell your callers you'll get back to them later. At other times of the day, you may want to take the important calls and return the calls of lesser importance when it's more convenient for you. Don't interrupt yourself by answering the phone and then telling the caller you're tied up and will have to call back.

Another time-saver is to let people know just when you're most likely to be available to take their calls. Simply telling people when they can usually reach you will save time on both ends of the line.

When a person you've been trying to reach returns your call and you happen to be in a meeting, you're faced with a difficult choice: "Do I interrupt the meeting and take the call (keeping several people waiting and wasting their time), or do I tell my secretary to take a message?" It's a tough decision, but usually you take the call.

There can be some very expensive consequences for allowing yourself to be interrupted in this manner. You've already been interrupted once by the announcement that somebody is on the phone. When you take the call, there's an even bigger disruption. The flow of your meeting is disturbed, and important points may not be discussed in complete detail, or may not be discussed at all.

The interruption also affects the people whose time is being wasted while you're on the phone. They have things to do, too, and they aren't getting them done. Their schedule as well as yours is being disrupted. It's also rude and insulting to take telephone calls during a meeting.

Unless it's a genuine emergency, don't allow yourself to be interrupted by a phone call. Have someone take a message; you can call back later. It's far better to keep even an important caller waiting for a few minutes than to waste your colleagues' time and risk causing their resentment and irritation.

Calls That Won't End

Every once in a while, we get calls that just won't end. Some people seem to talk forever, and you can waste a half hour every time they call. Here are some ideas that may work for you:

- Tell them at the start of the conversation that you were just walking out the door and only have a minute.
- Say you have someone in your office, so the conversation will have to be short.
- Tell them you have to take a call on the other line.
- When the conversation begins to drag, tell them you have a meeting that's about to start and you must go.
- If all else fails, hang up on yourself (in mid-sentence). Since the conversation was basically over, they'll think there was a problem with the phones and won't call back.

There are lots of polite excuses for terminating endless phone calls—or not taking them in the first place. Here are a few of the latter you can have your secretary or receptionist use:

- "I'm sorry, he's in a meeting."
- "He's on the other line."
- "He just stepped out of the office."

We've all heard these excuses, and we all use them, even if sometimes they aren't the truth. Your time is important, and you should try to reduce the number of phone calls that interrupt or waste it. But it's also important to be polite. When you get a message to call someone you don't really want to talk to, return the call anyway, or have your secretary call on your behalf. If you don't, there's a pretty good chance that the unwanted caller will call again.

There are some people who never return calls. They seem to think that being unreachable makes them more important. I wonder how they stay in business. Then there are others who are brusque or rude and give the impression that they just can't be bothered. I'd rather give the impression that I'm available and interested, no matter who the caller is, even if it takes a few extra minutes. In the long run, it's better for your reputation and more valuable for your business.

You can be efficient in handling your phone calls without being deficient in courtesy. Remember the ancient proverb: "Talk on the phone unto others as you would have them talk on the phone unto you."

17

Put It in Writing

Rely on notes, not your memory

The single most important timesaving technique to learn is to *write it down*. You may have a very good memory, but why burden yourself with trying to remember more than you have to? Thanks to the invention of the pencil and paper, there really isn't any reason to remember anything. Think with a pencil in your hand. Put your thoughts on paper, and you'll eliminate the need to remember them. All you have to remember now is where you put the paper.

We've already solved the paper problem with the creation of your Master List and Master Files. Here's the procedure:

- Keep track of all your ongoing projects by writing them on your Master List. Keep the list up to date.
- All the information that relates to these projects belongs in the appropriate folder, which you store in your Master File.

- Write your thoughts and ideas on paper and put them in the appropriate file.
- All important dates and deadlines that concern your ongoing projects should also be written on your calendar.

Meetings and Telephone Calls

It's particularly important to write down your thoughts, observations, and comments after a meeting or telephone call. With the passage of time, memories tend to blur. It's tough trying to remember conversations or discussions that took place months ago. If you write down what was said or what is to be done and by what date, you'll have a complete record. It's a wonderful way to stay on top of everything. In fact, you may be the only person taking notes during the meeting, and that could be very helpful to you later.

- Keep a continuous record of your conversations with clients or customers. With time, you'll see patterns develop that could be very helpful in your future dealings.
- Record the dates of your telephone conversations and the times at which you attempted to reach someone but weren't successful.
- Write down the name of the person's secretary or assistant when you call. Calling that person by name is a very nice touch.

When you write everything down, you'll find your memory improves because you're keeping more accurate and thorough notes and records on paper instead of inside your head.

Date Your Papers

Every time you make a note on a piece of paper, put a date on it. Sometimes the chronology of events can be very important and meaningful. By dating your notes and papers, you can see how things have changed or progressed with time. It will also allow you to follow the evolution of your thinking and see how your ideas have grown and developed.

Record Telephone Numbers

When you look up a telephone number, write it down. Put the name and number in your address book, Rolodex, the appropriate file, or all three, if necessary. The time it takes will be more than made up by the time you save by not having to search for the information when you next need it. Don't write the number on a scrap of paper or the back of an envelope. You'll lose it or it'll end up with the scraps of paper all over your desk.

It sounds simple, doesn't it? And it really is! But there's one habit that can gum up the works. It's called *scratchpaditis*.

It's always a good idea to have a scratch pad or a yellow legal pad at your elbow to take notes of telephone conversations or jot down thoughts or ideas. But if you're like most people, after a while that pad is full of dates, telephone numbers, random notes, and maybe even grocery lists—all decorated by doodles. You've got a case of scratchpaditis, and trying to find a name or number you need, or recall an important thought, is like looking for a needle in a haystack.

Another form of scratchpaditis is jotting something down on a piece of paper and then tucking it into your pocket. When you need it again, it's in your other suit, or may have already gone to the dry cleaner.

A related ill is *curly-scratchpaditis*. You make notes on a pad and then curl the paper over the top so that you can write on a fresh sheet. Before long you end up with pages and pages of meticulous notes, all still attached to the pad. No wonder you can't find that important name or number, or the reminder of an important project, even if you did write them down. Since all the pages remain on the pad, everything is either forgotten or buried in a very curly pad.

There *is* a cure. If you insist on filling page after page of your scratch pad, don't curl them over. Tear off each page as soon as it's full. Then, at some point during the day—this is crucial—go through all the pages that have accumulated and separate your notes. Those that pertain to ongoing projects should be transferred to a single sheet of paper, preferably the standard 8½-by-11 size, and placed in the appropriate folder in your Master File. Update your Master List, if necessary, from that jumble of notes. Enter names, addresses, and telephone numbers in your address book or Rolodex. Note deadlines on your calendar. Cross out each item on that page of your scratch pad as you dispose of it, and then throw the page away. It's like cleaning out your dresser drawers. Get rid of the stuff you don't need and organize the stuff you do need, so that you'll know where to find it.

It may be impossible to avoid making notes on little bits of paper, a napkin, or even the back of a business card if you happen to be in someone else's office, at a restaurant, or walking down the street when an idea hits you. If you tuck these notes into your pocket, make sure you take them out at the end of the day and put them where they belong.

Of course, the ideal cure for scratchpaditis is to write your notes on separate pieces of paper and place them in the appropriate file immediately. If you're a doodler, why not keep a separate scratch pad at hand for that specific purpose? If you can't cure scratchpaditis, you can at least keep it under control. You'll save yourself time and a lot of aggravation.

One last word of caution: When you're making notes, whether on a scratch pad, a separate piece of paper for your files, or even the back of an envelope, use only *one side*. If you use both sides, the odds are 50-50 that you'll lose, forget, or throw away the information that's on one of them.

Don't worry about putting a big piece of paper with only one small note on it inside your Master File. First of all, that piece of paper won't get lost or crushed by the other papers in your file. Second, it gives you the space to

enter more information whenever you open that file. Besides, when you're working with that file later, you'll have the opportunity to consolidate all the notes you've accumulated and throw away anything you don't need anymore.

There's one final—but big—plus to writing everything down. Not only is it a time-saver and a memory refresher for you, it creates a good impression on others. You're attentive, you're organized and efficient, and you're serious enough about your job to commit everything to writing. You'll also help keep the people you work with on their toes when they realize they're not talking into thin air. Their words are being preserved for posterity by the thin lead of your pencil.

18

Tools of the Trade

*How to use calendars, address books, and
other office organizers*

Calendars, address books, Rolodexes, and appointment
books are the usual tools of the office trade. They serve
primarily to keep you organized and on time, and to remind you of appointments, meetings, and deadlines. But
like any tool, they should be used for the purpose for which
they were designed. You don't pound in a nail with a screw-
driver. So why use your calendar to jot down names, telephone numbers, or notes that you'll want to keep long after
the calendar is out of date?

For some reason, many people like to stuff their address
book and Rolodex with more information than they can
conveniently hold. I've seen Rolodexes that were so full
you could hardly separate the cards enough to read them.
All these office tools are supposed to make your life and
your job easier, not more difficult. And they will—and save
you a lot of time to boot—if you use them properly.

Your Calendar

Here are some thoughts on how to use your calendar more effectively:

- Your calendar should be the last thing you look at when you leave the office each evening and the first thing, along with your Master List, that you look at when you arrive in the morning.

- Use your calendar in close conjunction with your Master List. Schedule appointments with yourself and write them on your calendar. If you start a project and you don't complete it, schedule another appointment with yourself and write it on your calendar for a future day.

- Throughout the day make new entries as appointments are scheduled or you undertake new projects. Block out time for yourself before someone else takes it. Then you'll have at your fingertips a reminder of both your daily and weekly agenda.

- Use a calendar that displays at least a week at a time. If you schedule a lot of meetings and appointments, consider one that shows a month at a time. With a flip of a page or two, you can see your agenda for the coming weeks. If you're looking for a reminder of something you did in the past, just flip the pages in the other direction.

- Don't use a calendar that shows only a day or two at a time. You may forget what meetings you've scheduled for tomorrow or the day after until you've flipped the pages.

- Don't use a calendar that requires you to tear off the page every day or even every week. Anything you wrote on those pages will be

long gone if you need it in the future, and
you'll lose a valuable record of your past activities.

- If you carry your calendar with you, leave a
photocopy of it on your desk or with your
secretary. That way your office always knows
where you are.

- Always keep one calendar, and one only.
There is an old Chinese proverb: "A man who
has two watches never knows the correct
time." If you keep a calendar in your briefcase
and another stays on your desk, there may be
something scheduled on one that doesn't get
written in the other.

- Always use a pencil. When meetings are
changed, you can erase that entry instead of
scratching it out with your pen. Otherwise
your calendar will look messy, and you won't
even be able to read it.

- Don't use your calendar to jot down names,
telephone numbers, or notes that you'll want
to keep. Write these notes on a piece of paper
and put it in the appropriate file.

- Your calendar will be most useful if you think
of it as a mini–time log. Just enter the major
items on your agenda: important deadlines,
meetings, ongoing projects, and the like. Keep
it as a permanent record.

Your Appointment Book

The difference between an appointment book and a calendar is that the former should give you a fairly detailed
picture of what you have to do and where you'll be during
the course of any given day—scheduled right down to the
minute, if necessary. And its advantage over a calendar is

that you can take it with you when you leave the office.
Here are some tips on how to use your appointment book
most efficiently:

- Use an appointment book that contains only a
  single month. There's no need to carry a whole
  year around with you. That's a waste of space
  and effort. Toward the end of the month, carry
  both the current and future month with you,
  so that you can schedule upcoming appointments. That's still better than a much bigger
  book.

- An appointment book that's small enough to
  fit inside a pocket or a purse is virtually useless. And if it shows a month at a time, you'll
  need a magnifying glass to read it. Use a book
  that's big enough to provide plenty of space for
  numerous entries, but small enough to fit into
  your briefcase or travel bag. You should also
  have the space to write the address and telephone number of the person you're meeting.

- You can use your appointment book to note
  down out-of-pocket expenses. It's even a good
  place to tuck the receipts you need for your
  expense account. Just don't leave them there.
  Put them in the appropriate folder when you
  return to the office.

- You may want to give your secretary or assistant permission to make appointments for you
  and enter them in the book. If you're out of
  the office or traveling, your appointment book
  will show your colleagues where you are and
  how you can be reached—provided, of course,
  you don't take it with you. If you do, naturally
  you should give the details of your itinerary to
  whoever might need them.

- If you have both an appointment book and a calendar, you can leave your calendar at your office. It's great insurance against the catastrophe of losing the appointment book. It's also a good practice to let people in your office know what your schedule will be for the following day. Then they will know when you're expected in the office or where you can be reached.

Your appointment book can serve two other very useful functions. It's a potent reminder *not* to overschedule your day. Meetings almost always run a little long. It takes time to get from one place to another, even from one office to another within your own company. There are bound to be delays, interruptions, or even emergencies that can throw an overcrowded schedule right out the window. It's probably a natural tendency to overload our schedules—we don't want to waste time—but when you see a page of your appointment book beginning to look crowded, with very little breathing space in between the entries, resist the temptation to squeeze in just one more appointment. You might be late or even have to cancel. Schedule that meeting for another day that isn't so crowded.

Your appointment book will also remind you of one of the most important rules of business: *Confirm all your appointments.* That's why you should always enter a name and number in your book right next to the time of the meeting.

Confirm all your appointments before you walk out the door. You'll reduce the risk of being kept waiting or stood up completely. It's almost impossible to keep to a schedule because of the unexpected emergencies and crises that arise. Almost everybody runs late; meetings are delayed or postponed. If you don't call first, you run the risk of wasting a half hour in a reception room or, worse, learning that the appointment won't be kept at all.

Unfortunately, people don't always extend the courtesy of calling to let you know that a meeting will be delayed or even canceled. It's a very frustrating experience and a terrible waste of your precious time. It can all be avoided by a little common courtesy on one side and a polite request for confirmation on the other. When you schedule an appointment, leave your phone number and ask that you be notified well ahead of time if there will be any change. If the day of the appointment arrives and you haven't been called, you are faced with two possibilities: either everything is still scheduled as planned, or—and this is far more likely—nobody has been thoughtful enough to inform you that there's been a change. That's when you jump into action and pick up the phone. Here are some guidelines:

- When you've scheduled early-morning appointments, call the afternoon before to confirm. Leave your home phone number if you won't be at your office before the time of the meeting.
- Monday morning meetings are often forgotten. Assume that the person you're meeting won't check his calendar on Friday afternoon and may forget the Monday morning meeting. Call him on Friday as a reminder. Or you may want to leave your home phone number in case there's a last-minute change in plans.
- If your time is billable, charge a cancellation fee to people who don't give you adequate notice. They'll be more considerate in the future—time is money.
- When you're the one who's running late, call to say that you'll be there soon. That way you'll know whether the meeting can still take place or has to be rescheduled. Call ahead and

you won't waste your time rushing to a meeting that won't be held.

Calling to confirm any appointment is a kind of insurance. Remember, almost half of your scheduled meetings will be canceled or postponed. Use your appointment book as your insurance policy. It's all right there: where to call, whom to call, and what number to call. You'll find this is one kind of insurance that really pays off.

Your Rolodex

- Is your Rolodex suffering from a severe case of obesity?
- Have you been putting names, addresses, and phone numbers into your Rolodex for years without taking any out?
- Is your Rolodex so full you can't push the cards far enough apart to read them?
- Do your Rolodex cards look like the Rosetta stone?

If your answer to any of these questions is yes, why not take a few minutes and go through the cards, throw the old ones away, and rewrite the ones you want to keep? There are certainly a lot of people in there you haven't talked to or done business with in years. Their cards are just taking up space. As for the ones you can barely read because the person has changed jobs so many times, make up a new one with the current information on it. Here are a few tips:

- Be consistent in how you lay out the information on your cards.
- The telephone number is the piece of information you will probably need to find most often.

It should be at the top of the card. Your card should look something like this:

Smith, John J.   (312) 444-2200
ABC Manufacturing Corp.
Regional Vice President
1200 North State Street
Chicago, IL 60660

- Attach the person's business card to the Rolodex card. Why bother to copy it, when the card has all the information you need? Use Scotch tape instead of staples (they take up more space). Make sure all the business cards are facing the same direction. Circle the phone number so that it's easy to see.
- Don't use the colored plastic covers. They take up space and create more busywork.
- Remove the blank cards from the Rolodex. Leave just a few at the back of the card file and put the rest in a drawer.

When you've finished the job, you'll have a slimmer, trimmer Rolodex. Now you can use this tool as it was meant to be used, with the card you're referring to lying flat and all the information clearly visible.

Your Address Book

A Rolodex *and* an address book? Isn't that overkill? It is if you never leave your office. But if you do, it can come in handy. Most of us carry around a little personal address book with important names and numbers. Why not a similar book for important business names and numbers?

- Use a business address book big enough to read easily but small enough to carry with you whenever you'll need it outside the office. You could probably compile one very quickly by just flipping through your Rolodex. You can also use it to enter new names and numbers when you're out of the office.

- Don't make the mistake of relying solely on an address book. If your whole business life is enclosed in this little book, if all your contacts, suppliers, and customers are written on these pages, you'll be in *big* trouble if you lose it.
- Be sure to periodically update your Rolodex files, or whatever system you have in the office for keeping track of names and addresses, by adding the new entries from your address book, or photocopy the book. That's another little bit of insurance against a lot of potential problems.

There are scores of other office aids available. Office-supply stores are full of them, though in my opinion some are more impressive-looking than useful. I've described the ones I think will both save you time and keep you organized. You can use any other system you like, as long as it accomplishes the same essential purposes. There's just one precaution: If you find you're spending a lot of time keeping yourself organized with diaries, work logs, tickler files, and leather-bound ledgers, then you're wasting the time you should be using to get your real work done. Have you ever heard of the KISS Principle? It means "Keep It Simple, Sweetheart."

19

Go with the Flow

Save time handling routine paperwork and correspondence

Handling routine paperwork and correspondence can be a time-consuming business these days. Just the sheer volume of paper that flows in and out of most offices can cause a problem. The trick is to go with the flow so that your paperwork, whatever its volume, doesn't back up, pile up, or spill over.

Sift and Sort

Most of us have "in" and "out" boxes. Where are yours kept? If they're on your desktop, move them to another location, preferably out of sight and out of easy reach. That serves several useful purposes. It will give you more desk space. You won't be disturbed or interrupted every time someone picks something up or leaves something off. And you won't be tempted to stop whatever you're doing to take a look at what just arrived.

The functions of your "in" and "out" boxes are self-explanatory. Nothing should stay in either one for very long. Here are my recommendations for how to keep paperwork moving:

- Set aside a specific time each morning and afternoon to deal with incoming paperwork. When that time comes, put your "in" box in the middle of your desk and start going through everything that has arrived since you last went through it. Look at each piece of paper, report, document, or whatever it is and decide *immediately* what to do with it. If there's work to do, write it on your Master List and place the information in the appropriate folder in your Master File. If you don't need to keep the paper or send it on, throw it out.
- If you can get rid of something in just a few seconds, do it. Sign it, send it on to someone else—whatever has to be done—and put it in your "out" box. If it requires more than a few seconds of your time, note it on your Master List and put the paper in the appropriate file. If you spend even a few minutes to handle more than just a routine task right then, you'll never get through your "in" box. A letter or memo that requires only a brief reply can be dealt with on the spot. Write directly on the piece of paper, or use a Post-it note, and send it on.

Reports, memos, periodicals, printouts, and anything else that you have to spend some time reading should be kept in a folder. Don't be tempted to start looking at them now. Using this very simple sifting-and-sorting process, you'll have an empty "in" box in a matter of minutes, and nothing will be buried when it begins to fill up again.

Magazines and journals should be separated from other

paperwork and put in a "Things to Read" folder or placed in your briefcase to be read at home, if that's your usual practice. Correspondence that requires a reply can go into a file folder until you have time to deal with several letters at once. Items that can be delegated or must be discussed with someone else can also go into a folder. If you jump up every time you want to talk to someone or pass along a piece of routine paperwork, you're interrupting yourself, and you become fair game for "just one quick question."

Never handle routine items one at a time. But always note the dates on the paperwork you're accumulating. If it's more than a week old, that's a pretty good sign you'd better start thinking about a time to do whatever has to be done.

The rationale behind this sifting-and-sorting process is simple. You can immediately get rid of or pass on probably at least half of all the paperwork that comes to you. The rest has been sorted out, with similar jobs grouped together so that you can handle them together, not one at a time—a big time-saver.

The single most important rule to remember when dealing with routine paperwork is *don't add to it unnecessarily.* Be certain that everyone listed on a routing slip or memo actually should receive that material. Make sure you yourself are not receiving unnecessary papers just because your initials are on a routing slip.

Why write a memo or a report if a phone call will do? If you do write interoffice communications, keep them short and to the point. Sending more than one page almost guarantees that the response will be delayed. You'll be judged for efficiency not by the volume of the paperwork you create but by the volume you can handle.

Write a Letter—but Make It Short

The key to writing a good letter is giving yourself enough time to edit and revise it. The first draft doesn't have to be great, only the last one. It's very easy to write a letter that's several pages long, but it takes a lot of thought and effort to make that same letter only one page in length.

Whatever your system for writing letters, the most important thing to remember is to get that first draft completed as quickly as possible. It doesn't matter if you write it out longhand, use a tape recorder, or type it yourself on the P.C. Just plan to rewrite it two or three times before you mail it.

If someone types your letters for you, first have a double-spaced rough draft done, and then start editing. With the wonderful word-processing programs available now, it isn't very difficult to make the desired changes and corrections. If you prefer to do your writing in longhand, keep a legal pad in your briefcase and write your letters and memos while you're commuting to and from the office, waiting in an airport, or wherever you happen to have a spare moment.

If you don't use a portable tape recorder, you should give it a try. Taking dictation may not be the best use of a secretary's time. While you are dictating your letters and memos to a tape recorder, a secretary can be doing something more important. It may take you a while to get accustomed to using it—your voice on tape never sounds like your real voice—but it can save you a lot of time. You can dictate wherever you happen to be—in your office, at home, on an airplane, in a hotel room, and certainly in the back of a chauffeured limousine. All you need is a little privacy. No one wants to sit next to someone who's talking to a machine.

Once you get the hang of it, you can dictate memos, letters, notes, and instructions to your secretary or assistant, as well as to yourself. A tape recorder can prove invaluable when you're beginning a new project and want to record your thoughts and ideas. Of course, everything you dictate, even your notes to yourself, must be transcribed on paper and then put in the proper place. It always takes longer to listen than to read, and longer still if you have to play through a pile of cassettes to find what you're looking for.

Whatever system you use to handle routine paperwork and correspondence, the important thing is to be sure not to let the mundane aspects of your job interfere with its more creative and valuable functions. Routine jobs are just that—routine, like mowing the lawn. Do them on a regular basis, at times that won't interfere with your more productive work. If you let it go too long, the job will be twice as hard and time-consuming. Look at it this way: If you cut the grass one blade at a time, you'd never get the job done.

20

Read to Save Time—Save Time to Read

How to get your reading up to speed

We're all inundated with reading material—newspapers, magazines, trade journals, and lots of company reports and other information that accumulates in piles on our desks every day. If you don't read it all, you feel guilty because you want to be informed and there's always the possibility that you're missing something important. But if you took the time to read everything, you'd hardly have any time left for your real work. Change the *way* you read, and you'll get all the information you need and still save time. Here are some tips.

Newspapers

How do you read a newspaper? Front to back? Page by page? The sports, business, or features sections first, and then the rest? Try this:

- Flip through the entire paper page by page. Glance at each story, look at the headline, and read the first sentence or two.
- Ask yourself, "Is this something I want to read?" If so, pull out your pen (a red felt-tip pen will make that story jump out at you) and draw a big circle around the headline.
- If you write the page numbers on which the articles appear on the front of the newspaper, you won't have to hunt through the entire paper later.

Within about sixty seconds, you should be able to go through an entire newspaper, scanning each and every page and circling the things you want to look at or read. You can now determine where each article falls in relative importance.

- Read the most important articles first and the others later, when you have some free time.
- Tear out the pages or cut out the articles that you can't get to now, and throw the rest of the paper away. Place the clipped articles into your "Things to Read" folder and read them when you have a few extra minutes, or take the folder home and read the articles at night.

Magazines

Nothing accumulates faster than unread magazines. And, with the exception of newspapers, nothing goes out of date faster. By clipping articles you want to read, you'll save huge amounts of space and keep only the information that has lasting importance. When you receive a magazine, look first at the table of contents. Are there any articles that appear to be of interest? If so, take out a pen and circle the story's page number, or turn to the article and tear it out of the magazine. Staple the pages of the story together and throw the magazine away. You don't need it anymore. Put the article in your reading folder and look at it when you have a chance.

Many businesses subscribe to only one copy of a magazine and then route it around the office. Obviously you can't tear articles out of that. Often, though, a magazine will sit on someone's desk for weeks or months before he finally puts his initials on the routing slip and sends it on. By the time the magazine has completed its circulation, the information is old and stale.

Why not photocopy the table of contents and distribute it to everyone the day the magazine arrives? If there's an article that someone wants, he can circle it on the sheet, and the article will then be copied and given to him. That way everybody can have the desired information before it becomes hopelessly out of date.

Reports

When you receive a report or some other important inter-office communication, don't just put it aside with the intention of looking at it later. And don't drop whatever you're doing to read it at that very minute. Try this:

- Scan the report quickly to get an overview of what the information means and how important it is.
- Does it need to be addressed immediately, or can it wait a while?
- If it's important, write it on your Master List to be read and acted on at some time that you've set aside to deal with such reports.
- If it isn't all that important, place it in your reading folder and get to it later.

Scanning and sorting your reading material will help you cover a lot more ground in a lot less time. Here are some other time-savers:

- Are you a subscription junkie because your company pays for all your subscriptions? If so, you're probably wasting your time and your company's money. Ask yourself, "Would I subscribe to this magazine if I had to pay for it myself?" If the answer is no, cancel it.
- Take a few minutes to evaluate all the magazines and periodicals you receive—in terms of their importance to your job, not your reading pleasure. Read the most important ones and cancel the rest.
- Schedule a regular reading time as a part of your daily or weekly routine—perhaps with a coffee break in the morning, or as a break between intense work periods. If you scatter your reading throughout the day, you're probably using it as an excuse to postpone working on more-important projects. If you let it accumulate, eventually you'll just throw it away.
- Do your reading at home, or at times when it's inconvenient to do any other kind of work, such as while you're traveling or staying out of town, commuting, or waiting for an appointment. With a little thought and organization, your briefcase can become a very valuable mobile library.

Finally, when you're deciding what to read, try also to decide how much time to spend reading it. Don't waste time on anything of only marginal value to you and your job. Skip-read and skim if it's of some greater value. But if it's truly important and will require concentration and careful reading, give yourself that time. And don't leave it until the last minute. Underline, make notations in the margins, highlight important sections with a felt-tip marker. Diligent reading is often as essential to the successful completion of a project as any other form of organization and preparation. Time spent reading carefully, when it's necessary, is time well spent.

21

Get Off the Beaten Track

*Do things at times when nobody else
is doing them*

How much time do you waste every day standing in line? It's not only aggravating and frustrating, it can throw your schedule off completely. Once when I was complaining about a long line, I said, "There are too many people in this town." My friend disagreed. "That's not the problem," he said. "We're just all doing the same thing at the same time." I think he had a point.

Lunch

If you have lunch around noon like everybody else, you'll probably stand in line for fifteen or twenty minutes, even if you have a reservation. Why not eat early or late, at 11:30 A.M. or 1:15 P.M., when the restaurant is nearly empty and you can have any seat in the house? The time you would have wasted standing in line can be spent working at the office, and you can still have an enjoyable meal.

Banking

Have you ever tried to cash a check at noon on a Friday? How long did you stand in line? Fifteen, twenty minutes or more? Do you use cash machines? On Fridays the lines can be fifteen or twenty people long. Everybody needs money for the weekend. Eventually the machines run out of cash and you're out of luck—and have to stand in line at another machine. Do your banking early in the week. There aren't any lines. You're finished in a matter of minutes and are on your way.

Commuting

If you have the flexibility, try going to and from work when there isn't a lot of automobile traffic. It may mean getting up early to beat the rush, but then maybe you can also leave early to stay ahead of the afternoon rush hour. It takes some creative thinking, but you may be able to reduce your travel time by an hour a day. You can spend that time much more productively at the office than in your car.

If it's available, take public transportation to work instead of driving. Why should you spend up to an hour or more dodging traffic, with all the delays and aggravations that can cause, when you can spend the same amount of time on a bus or train, getting some reading or work done? Let someone else do the driving, and you'll arrive at your destination in a much more relaxed state of mind. You might also be able to schedule your commuting times to avoid the rush-hour peaks. That's even more relaxing.

Time you spend waiting, whether it's in traffic or in the pickup line at a deli, is wasted time. Whatever you have to do, don't do it when everybody else is doing the same thing.

22

On the Road Again

Staying in touch when you're out of town

If your job requires you to spend any amount of time out of town, you know the problems that business travel can create. First of all, there's that pile of unfinished work that will sit on your desk until you return. Then there's the work you're generating while you're out of town. And last but not least, new paperwork is piling up on your desk at the usual rate. Your first day back at the office is often a frantic race to catch up. It may be another day or two before you finally break even.

The telephone is not the only way you can stay in touch with your office while you're out of town. Through the use of portable tape recorders, express mail, fax machines, and lap-top computers, you can not only stay in touch, you can also stay on top of your work. When you finish a meeting or an appointment, make written notes or dictate your letters, memos, or reports while things are still fresh in your mind. Convert the otherwise wasted time spent in a taxi, at the airport, or in a hotel room into productive time. It isn't necessary to have a perfect letter or report. Just get your thoughts down so that you won't have to do it later. You can make the necessary changes after a draft is typed.

If you're on a long trip, you may want to express-mail tapes or any written material to your office so that it'll be typed and waiting for you when you return. Or you could use the secretarial services that many hotels now provide. The important thing is to take care of routine paperwork at least, so that you won't be swamped when you return.

Portable fax machines and lap-top computers now enable you to be in constant communication with your office wherever you are. The work that's sitting on your desk can be completed even though you're out of town. Overnight express mail is another way you can stay on top of your unfinished work. You can go through it when it arrives from your office, write the necessary instructions and replies, and then send it back that evening. That will keep the piles from accumulating.

You have to plan your business trips even more carefully than you would a routine day in the office if you really want to save time and money. Here are some tips:

- Prepare a detailed itinerary of both your business appointments and your overnight stays. Travel reservations, business meetings, and overnight accommodations should never be left to chance. Give a copy of your itinerary to the appropriate people at the office so that they'll know how to reach you.
- Allow plenty of time for travel between meetings and appointments. It may not be as easy getting from place to place in an unfamiliar city as you might think.
- Always confirm all your appointments as soon as you arrive at your destination. Your appointment book should contain the necessary

names, addresses, times, and telephone numbers.

■ Be flexible. Even the best-laid plans and schedules occasionally get off track. Instead of wasting your time fuming, use it productively by
catching up on your paperwork, your reading,
or even your telephone calls whenever you're
kept waiting in a reception room or an airport.

You should plan your return as carefully as you plan
your trip. It's usually not necessary to arrive back at the
office in the middle of the day. You're tired and may be
suffering from jet lag. You're not in the best shape to handle
the inevitable backlog of work. Go home and work there, if
necessary. Then get a good night's sleep. Arrive at the office
early the next day and schedule a stretch of uninterrupted
time, during your most productive work hours, so you'll be
able to catch up.

Better yet, *before* you go out of town, block out your
catch-up time on your calendar and leave specific instructions that nobody is to schedule any appointments for you
during that time. You'll find you'll be able to resume your
normal office routine with relative ease.

23

High-Tech Temptations

Timesaving—and time-wasting—
office machines

Do you ever long for the good old days, when the most complicated office machine was a typewriter? Now we have telephones with their own mini-switchboards, word processors, calculators, computers, electronic mail, voice mail, fax machines, beepers, mobile phones, duplicating machines, and even electric pencil sharpeners. Do they make work easier or more complicated? Do they save time or waste it?

That depends entirely on how they're used. There's no question that electronic office equipment, in the hands of properly trained operators, can be a big time-saver, in spite of the inevitable glitches and breakdowns. The question now becomes whether it is economical. Is the cost of the machines *plus* that of the trained operators worth it in terms of time saved and increased productivity? Every office situation is different, and only careful study can provide an answer. The real danger lies in falling victim to a smooth-talking salesman and installing expensive equipment that will be underutilized or will quickly become obsolete, and will never pay for itself.

But what about the office machines that are all too easy for *everybody* to use? I'm thinking in particular of copying machines. In the old days, the only way to duplicate a document was to type a carbon copy or cut a stencil for a mimeograph machine—a time-consuming and messy process. As a result, there wasn't much unnecessary duplication being done. Now, with just the touch of a button, you can have a hundred copies of everything in only a few minutes. The temptation is often too great to resist, and suddenly you've created mountains of paper and a lot of unnecessary paperwork.

Try to avoid that temptation. Every time you're on the way to the copier, ask yourself, "Is this trip really necessary?" If it is, make only the number of copies you *know* you need and send them *only* to the people who need to see them. Ask them to return the favor.

I'm all for tape recorders and pocket calculators. They really are time-savers. The fax machine is now in the process of revolutionizing business communications. That, too, will be a time-saver, although it may also generate a lot of unnecessary communications. As for the variety of telephone answering systems now in use, they can be a boon or a burden.

Many businesses have incorporated so-called voice mail into their telephone answering systems. You can now leave a detailed—and lengthy—message for the party you're trying to reach, at any time of day. The drawbacks are obvious. The caller has no written record of his call or of the information he wants to convey, unless his message is transcribed. Most often it's not; it's simply erased. In other words, it's always risky trusting a machine. Any important call should be followed up with a written communication if it isn't returned, or with additional calls until you finally reach a person, not a machine.

For the person who uses an answering machine to take his calls, it can be very time-consuming to have to listen to many taped messages. I would encourage you to suggest or even insist that callers limit their messages to the essentials: name, time, purpose of the call, the number where they can be reached, or the time they will call back. Then the tape can be reviewed quickly and the necessary names and numbers jotted down. Another time-saver for both caller and callee is to prepare what you're going to say when you know you're about to talk to a machine. Speak slowly and distinctly, and keep your message brief.

I have a philosophy about missed telephone calls. If it's important, the person will call back. Obviously, though, I'm the exception. Most people these days are afraid to be out of touch or out of reach for even a minute. Calls to and from cars, boats, and airplanes are no longer a rarity. I have a friend who has gone one step further. He recently decided to take up bicycling. The first thing he bought was a portable phone; a beeper wasn't enough. He plans to take long bicycle rides and is now thinking about buying a portable fax machine. From the ludicrous to the sublime . . .

24

Beat the Clock

How to give yourself more time to think

When you work more efficiently, you can work more productively. But the time you save can also be used in another important way. You can give yourself more time to think, plan, and contemplate a problem before you make a decision. The more time you spend thinking about a project or a problem, the better your chances of making great decisions.

Business has become so hectic and fast-paced that many times we are expected to make a decision simply because we have received some information on the fax machine. Information travels so fast and is so readily available that we often find ourselves inundated and overwhelmed. We're being forced to make decisions without having had the opportunity to "sleep on it."

In ancient times (the early '80s), if the person you were having a phone conversation with wanted to send you some additional information, it would take several days for the letter to arrive. That gave you some time to think. Today the person asks for your fax number, and the material is sent and received within seconds. And you're expected to respond immediately.

You need to give yourself more time to think before you respond or make a decision. You'll find this all-important thinking time in the many minutes you've saved by streamlining your office routines. You'll have the time to absorb all the information you've received. You'll have the time you need to look at a situation from a lot of different perspectives, trying to find all the holes. You'll have the time to search and explore in order to ensure that nothing has been overlooked. The likelihood of making sound business decisions always increases when you give yourself time to think.

There's another way you can find some creative thinking time. When I say, "Give me some time to sleep on it," I mean that literally. Good ideas can sometimes spring out of nowhere. A solution to a problem may suddenly pop into your head when you're relaxing, or thinking about something else, or even sleeping.

The fact is, when you become deeply involved with a project, you never really stop thinking about it. While you're doing something else, your mind will continue to flash back and forth between whatever you're presently involved with and the problem you're trying to solve. You may even discover the solution while you're asleep. A Nobel Prize was awarded to a scientist who pictured the configuration of a DNA molecule in a dream.

Always keep a pad of paper by your bed. When you do have these creative ideas, make sure you write them down. Then you can go back to sleep without worrying that you'll have forgotten your idea by the morning. If you're really inspired, get out of bed and work for an hour. Burning a bit of midnight oil can often pay off, saving time and increasing your productivity during the daylight hours.

You can do some of your most creative thinking when

you're away from the office, doing something else. That's another advantage of working efficiently during the hours you do spend at the office. You'll find more time for relaxation and other activities in your personal life, and you'll get a good—and possibly even a creative—night's sleep.

25

Quality Time

Time saved at work is time for yourself

The time has come to put all these ideas, concepts, and techniques to use. Make the most of them. Bend, shape, and mold them to fit your own needs, work style, office environment, habits, and personality. I guarantee they will save you time.

In today's business climate, every company is trying to improve the productivity of its employees. Corporations expect the maximum contribution from everybody. Your challenge is to demonstrate new ways in which you're helping the company make more money or reduce costs, thereby improving productivity. Your daily objective should be to get as much important work done as possible, in the shortest possible time. Your reward will be more time to enjoy the fruits of your hard work.

Schedule your days and weeks so that you start every day with a big bang. Once you get rolling and develop momentum, you won't slow down. Imagine scoring ten runs in the first inning of a baseball game. It makes the rest of the game a lot easier to win. Have a great Monday and Tuesday, and the rest of the week takes care of itself. It's much easier going through life if you're ahead than if you're always trying to catch up.

Make the projects that are of the greatest value to your company your number-one priority, both in time and effort. Don't procrastinate. Stay on track by minimizing interruptions, unnecessary meetings, and busywork. Think of yourself as part of a team—a winning team. And remember, when you save time at work, it's time you can use for yourself. You'll have more of it to spend with family and friends. You won't have to miss that ball game or movie. You'll have time to celebrate that birthday or anniversary and enjoy all the wonderful things life has to offer. Great things can happen when you have more time to spend on yourself. Get organized and you'll see marvelous changes in both your professional *and* your personal life. I guarantee it.

Acknowledgments

A big thank-you goes to all the people who helped me develop these ideas, techniques, and concepts.

A special thank-you goes to Fred Hills and Burton Beals, whose knowledge, training, and experience helped me shape my thoughts and ideas. It couldn't have been done without you.

MONEY-BACK GUARANTEE

We are so confident that this book will help you save time that we will send you a 100% refund if it doesn't. If you're not satisfied, send the book back to us* with your sales receipt and a note telling us why this book did *not* help you save time, and we'll reimburse you for the book, plus tax, as registered on the sales receipt.

Guarantee expires Aug. 31, 1991

Limited Warranty: This warranty gives you specific legal rights. You may also have other rights which vary from state to state.

*Simon & Schuster Distribution Center
Dept 220-12th Floor
1230 Avenue of the Americas
New York, NY 10020

Speeches and Seminars

Jeffrey J. Mayer would be delighted to speak at your next business meeting, or convention. For date availability, contact him at Mayer Enterprises.

Thoughts and Comments

If you would like to offer your thoughts or comments about this book, address them to the author at:

Mayer Enterprises
50 East Bellevue Place
Chicago, Il. 60611